WOMAN FOR PEACE

Woman for Peace

The Life of

BERTHA VON SUTTNER

By

Beatrix Kempf

translated from the German

by R. W. Last

NOYES PRESS

Noyes Building
Park Ridge, New Jersey 07656, U.S.A.

First U.S. Edition: 1973
Copyright © 1972 by Oswald Wolff Ltd., London
Library of Congress Catalog Card No.: 72–87475
ISBN: 0–8155–5013–8
Printed in Great Britain

CONTENTS

The Writings of Bertha von Suttner

*Translated by T. Holmes. See Sources to the Translations.

FOREWORD

It was by chance that my attention was drawn to the wealth of material left by Bertha Freiin von Suttner, the famous but none the less little known authoress, propagandist and campaigner for the peace movement, which is preserved in the Library of the United Nations in Geneva but has still to be studied in any depth. I began to take a deeper interest in this personality who even today is the object of such conflicting opinions; and what I discovered proved to be of such considerable interest that I resolved to make the attempt to present a picture of the life of this extraordinary woman, basing my study on the diaries, letters, speeches, etc., preserved in the Geneva archives.

I wish to thank the Federal Ministry of Education for their support and practical help in making it possible for some of the documents to be brought to Vienna for me to examine them here. I wish to express my gratitude also to the generosity of the Theodor Körner foundation, whose award made it possible for me to travel to Geneva to conclude my work there and investigate the library's archive holdings. I owe a particular debt of thanks to the Principal Librarian of the Library of the United Nations in Geneva, Dr. A. C. Breycha-Vauthier, who obtained these documents for Geneva, because as a result of his initiative the material is collected in one place and available to all. His profound knowledge of the subject and of the material were of the greatest assistance to me. The Nobel Foundation in Stockholm has also greatly assisted me by placing at my disposal photocopies of Bertha Suttner's letters to Alfred Nobel.

With all this generous assistance I was able to write the biography of this interesting and important Austrian lady, who exploited her knowledge of the intellectual and political trends of her age in order to seek ways and means of leading Europe out of its predominant nationalism into a federation of states, into a united Europe.

There is a direct link between the ideas and objectives of the peace movement, for which Bertha Suttner worked and propagandised, and those of organisations like the Interparliamentary

Union, the International Court at The Hague, the League of Nations, the United Nations, and many more. Those in blissful ignorance of her links with such international agencies still frequently mock Bertha Suttner as the "Bertha of Peace", and her enormous efforts and positive achievements in respect of these goals have gained scant recognition even today.

It is not widely known that Bertha Suttner kept Alfred Nobel constantly informed of her activities on behalf of the peace movement, nor that the section of his famous will which resulted in the institution of the Nobel Peace Prize can be traced back directly to her influence.

Virtually no one of the present generation is aware of the fact that Bertha Suttner was not just an accomplished journalist, but one of the very first women political journalists of all time, a woman who in addition was an outstanding propagandist for her ideas and her peace movement, which she championed with all the vigour her deep convictions bestowed upon her.

The Life of Bertha von Suttner

INTRODUCTION

Bertha Suttner died a few short weeks before the outbreak of the First World War. This "most popular lady", the best-known Austrian woman of the pre-war era, famous far beyond the confines of the Austrian empire, was fêted by her friends as a writer, honoured as a campaigner for the idea of peace, and loved as a kind and generous individual. Her enemies, on the other hand, attacked her with extreme viciousness, mocking her as a "peace suffragette" and cruelly caricaturing her as a "Bertha of Peace" brandishing her palm leaves of victory. Kings received her in audience, princes invited her as their guests, and she was in regular and lively correspondence with many of the principal personalities on the European political scene; yet she extended her friendship without prejudice to all who shared her views and who, like herself, were campaigning for the realisation of peace throughout the world. She was the first ever woman—and to this day the only Austrian woman—to be accorded the Nobel Peace Prize, which her friendship with Nobel had been instrumental in establishing.

She must have been a remarkable woman indeed to have succeeded in playing such an influential role at a time when women enjoyed few of the rights they have today. For, although as a writer, she produced no works of any great literary merit, she was able, by means of a single novel, a series of articles and lectures, and above all else through the power of her personality and the great vigour with which she expressed her convictions, to exercise a determining influence on international institutions and organisations, and to win over to her cause great names in the fields of politics, science, literature and the arts.

Bertha Suttner's endeavours on behalf of the peace movement, which constituted a political career and established her fame, began in the year 1886 and ended only with her death on 21 June 1914. So she was active in an age marked by the division of Europe into the Triple Alliance and the Entente. It was a time of great advances in science and technology which had aroused in many people the hope that ever closer international co-operation among scientists would bring in its train similar collaboration among politicians. Democratic socialism with its international proclivities turned into a force to be reckoned with. It now seemed possible to defeat outmoded nationalism by building bridges across state frontiers. A federation of European states into an international union, a "United States of Europe", was no longer thought to be a mere pipe dream; and people really believed they were already on the way towards this promised land.

But at the same time the nationalists were becoming more and more influential and determining the policies of the great European powers. Nationalists and internationalists of all political complexions were increasingly coming into conflict. Disputes between the supporters of one philosophy and the other became more and more intense, whether they called themselves monarchists or socialists, militarists or pacifists, or anything else under the sun. It was a bitter conflict which was never finally resolved; and even today it continues to figure prominently in international politics. But over the debates and resolutions in the international conferences and congresses which had been so fashionable since the nineteenth century, just like those in the national parliaments and the international press, there hung the shadow of fear of a terrible war, of a collision between highly mechanised armies, and horror at the prospect of a catastrophe of immeasurable proportions.

In those years which are often so wrongly regarded as "peaceful", as the "good old days", the destiny of millions hung in the balance, not just the future of one generation, but of several generations in Europe, and indeed in the world at large. What fate held in store for them was the First World War, the defeat of the Central Powers and the peace treaties of Versailles and Saint-Germain. Hailed as a great victory for the idea of nationalism and implemented under the slogan "self-determination for individual peoples", the dissolution of the Austro-Hungarian monarchy brought new nation states into being, in which narrow chauvinism sparked off renewed international conflict, ultimately leading to the dictatorship of National Socialism which was finally brought to its knees in the Second World War only after enormous sacrifices in human life.

In 1918 and the inter-war years none of the international agencies proved powerful enough to turn the tide of history. After the Second World War, a great deal older and wiser, they took up their work again—although quite often under different names—but still dreaming the old dream of bringing peace to earth for all mankind.

Bertha Suttner's diary entries and articles reveal the intense interest with which she followed political events in Europe; she too recognised the mounting tensions which were building up an atmosphere of great uncertainty, of inevitable disaster. In her "Footnotes to Contemporary Affairs", which appeared in the journal *Die Friedens-Warte*, she sought to describe how she saw the dangerous game the politicians in power were playing. She warned in her speeches, writings and articles against the dangers of a war waged with modern weapons, and tried to make people aware that the disaster was imminent. She threw the whole weight of her personality behind her campaign, which she waged with untiring missionary zeal. Depending on the views of her listeners or readers, she either won loyal new supporters or was scorned. The events of the years that followed on her death, which overtook her a few days before the assassination of Franz Ferdinand, showed supporter and opponent alike that her acute mind and political instinct had accurately foreseen the tragedy of the coming decades.

Bertha Suttner the pacifist was not a visionary, nor did she have the delicate spirit of the romantic. By dint of intensive study she had acquired a profound knowledge of the manifold "isms" of her age. Right up until the end she noted down in her diaries the titles of the books she had selected for reading. Works of scholarship rubbed shoulders with modern literature. Every day she scanned the great English and French newspapers, as well as her own Austrian press. She conducted her campaign for the maintenance of peace with a wealth of background knowledge, and was thoroughly well informed on the political situation of the hour; as a result she was able to ward off all attacks against her that arose in discussion, to put forward her views on the basis of a knowledge of the facts, and often to take the offensive herself.

Among those who worked with her she was not regarded as "an artist of the first water, but as probably the most wide-ranging and knowledgeable among women writers",[1] as Leopold Katscher, secretary of the Austrian Peace Society, noted. Even today it is not easy to fit her into one of the normal pigeon-holes associated with lady writers, even though we have far more documentation on which to base our assessment than Katscher had. She was an accomplished writer, but not a great artist by comparison with her female contemporaries such as Clara Viebig and Gabriele Reuter. She was rather a first-rate journalist. She was not an active supporter of women's rights; the problems associated with the emancipation of women were of peripheral concern to her, despite the fact that she frequently found herself the only woman in the front line of attack. She was an aristocrat through and through, yet she was the severest critic of her own class. Among other things, she recognised the significance of socialism which in her eyes also had its clearly-defined limitations. In the fullest sense of the word she was a free human being, an independent spirit fighting against inherited prejudice, the "sacred cows" of the past, against anything that appeared detrimental, restrictive or outmoded. Despite her enthusiasms she acted and applied her judgement with great purposefulness and with an amazing lack of conventionality, even in her younger days. Filled with vigour and determination, she was mistress of herself and those about her. The fascination which her presence radiated must have been overwhelmingly great, to judge from letters written to her and the accounts of her contemporaries. Extraordinary though the personality of this woman was, her life was if anything even more extraordinary, lived out on a grand scale and filled with adventure.

NOTES

1. Leopold Katscher, Introduction to the complete edition of Bertha von Suttner's works, Dresden, 1906, vol. 1, p. xviii.

YOUTH

Bertha Freiin von Suttner was born on 9 June 1843 in Prague to Count Franz Joseph Kinsky von Wchinitz and Tettau deceased, former Feldmarschalleutnant in the imperial army, and Sophia Wilhelmine, née von Körner. On her father's side she belonged to a line of counts in the great Bohemian nobility which can be traced back to the twelfth century. A Count Kinsky was done to death in Eger with Wallenstein, another Kinsky wrote pedagogical treatises as Commandant of the Maria Theresa military academy in the Wiener Neustadt; and members of the princely line held the highest offices in the court of the Habsburgs. In his biographical dictionary of the Austrian empire, Wurzbach describes the house of Kinsky in his own antiquated style:

> Thus it is that the Kinskys are a quite remarkable family, wheresoever one might pursue their peregrinations; and there is not an indifferent member among them. Even when they take up arms against the existing order of things they can be reckoned great; their great energy and strength of conviction wins our due respect, if not our approbation.[1]

Bertha Suttner demonstrated that she placed great value on recognition of the fact that she belonged to the Kinsky line by quoting her baptismal certificate at the beginning of her memoirs, so that the world might know "where and when and in what setting I came into the world".[2]

The baptismal certificate also reveals that her mother had been the daughter of Captain of Horse Joseph von Körner—a relation of the freedom poet Theodor Körner—and that Count Kinsky had married a woman who, according to the codex of the Austrian high nobility, was not of equal rank, and this was not far short of being a mésalliance. His choice of wife caused his children to suffer many social disadvantages. Writing between 1906 and 1907, Bertha Suttner looked back in her old age at her first experiences in Viennese society:

> And now I was to come out into the world. Our name alone should have given us the right to move in the highest aristocratic

circles, for there wasn't a family in the Austrian nobility to which we were not related in some way or another. But anyone who thinks that name and connections are enough to guarantee acceptance has little knowledge of our aristocracy. One of the prerequisites—this is how it was in my young days, but now it is not so exclusive—was a direct line of sixteen forebears, that is, right to presentation at court. And that was something we did not possess.[3]

And a few lines further on, she continues :

A party among the nobility. I entered the ballroom filled with happy expectations. I left it hurt and disappointed. Only a few offered to dance with me. The matrons of the nobility sat together; my mother sat apart. The countesses stood around in small groups, chatting among themselves, but I knew none of them. During supper the company formed into gay little knots, but I was left out of it.[4]

The bitter tone in which she relates the experience of so many years before shows how deeply it affected her and what a crucial effect it was to have on the rest of her life. Being "left out of it" must have occasioned her a great deal of suffering, and time and again in her works she sets men of integrity and noble character in contrast to types drawn from aristocratic society as depicted in every novel of social criticism written at that time. One example of this comes in her early novel *High Life*, in which an American, having befriended a member of the German aristocracy, travels across Europe as a sharp critic of European conditions in general and the Austrian nobility in particular : "I found the English nobility proud, the French vain, but the Austrian arrogant in the extreme."[5]

Mother and daughter Kinsky must have drawn the logical conclusion from those bitter experiences with Viennese society, as they no longer wintered in the imperial city but in Venice, which in the early sixties still belonged to Austria, and also in Rome and Paris, where the people do not appear to have been so exclusive. Abroad they found the entrée to international society which they so desired.

Her mother's passion for gambling frequently led them to visit the fashionable German spas; but more often than not heavy losses caused them to interrupt their stay prematurely. As time went past their financial position worsened, and after a few years of travelling and playing the tables the entire fortune had been exhausted. Even before Countess Kinsky's experimentations in

* *

the gaming rooms had come to such a disastrous end, the young Bertha had taken up singing lessons with a view to embarking on a career as a singer. But despite her talent she was terribly nervous of an audience; and her voice was not powerful enough to be heard properly in a large hall. Her efforts to secure an engagement through an impressario, which her memoirs describe with gentle irony, did not meet with success; so this plan, whose object was to release them from financial embarrassment, foundered, and she had to abandon the idea of playing an important role in the "big world", if only as a singer.

Several suitors had asked the young countess for her hand in marriage, but they were refused; the three bethrothals mentioned in her memoirs came partly to a tragi-comic, partly to a tragic end. Once when she was still quite a young girl she had fallen in with the family's wishes and became engaged to a much older man, a rich industrialist, but she fled after the first kiss. The second time was in Paris, where she was promised to an Englishman; but happily he made himself scarce before the actual wedding—he was an adventurer whose supposed Australian fortune turned out to be a product of his fertile imagination. On the third occasion she promised to marry a Prince Wittgenstein. He was a gifted singer, and their love of music constituted a strong bond between them. During a crossing to the United States, where he hoped to gain artistic and financial success in an important concert tour, he fell ill suddenly and died before he could succeed in his plans and marry his countess.

After the tragic outcome of this engagement, which also marked the end of the somewhat aimless peregrinations of mother and daughter, the Kinsky family seems to have intervened with determination. The two of them were given the chance to settle in Görz, a small town in the monarchy, with an appropriate annual settlement. Arthur Kinsky, who had left the army prematurely because of a lung condition (army life had not appealed to him anyway), had moved some time previously to Split in Dalmatia. Bertha's mother concurred, and she begged her daughter to remain with her, or at least to resume her career as an artist. But Bertha preferred to seek a mode of employment which would enable her to earn a living immediately. "I wanted to see the world, and I wanted to have some kind of employment."[6] Thus it was that she entered the nouveau riche household of Freiherr von Suttner,[7] and became governess and companion to his four daughters and, two years later, against his wishes and those of his wife, married their third and youngest son, Arthur Gundaccar, Baron Suttner.

That was the day on which Bertha Suttner came out into the world, experiencing the pure joys of a happy marriage and later the profoundest grief of widowhood, and playing her part in the great issues of the day; I am still that Bertha Suttner, whereas the Bertha Kinsky, whom I have been writing about up to now, is like a figure in a picture book to me. I can remember her experiences in general terms, but they no longer move me.[8]

That is how she describes it in her memoirs, in that rather pathos-ridden style so characteristic of the seventies and eighties of the last century which can render her works somewhat hard to read today.

In looking back over her youth, she recognises the crucial significance for her life as a whole of her connexion with the Suttner family and the complete break with the past that this represented. The first period of her life, which came to an end when she entered the Suttner family, no longer appeared to her as a wasted time, but rather as a period of preparation for the work that lay before her. In her first thirty years, most of which she had spent abroad, in Paris, Rome, Venice, Baden-Baden, Wiesbaden, and elsewhere, she had not only acquired an exceptional knowledge of languages but had also had the opportunity to meet personally a whole range of important figures in international society, and both of these things stood her in good stead in later years. Her life was not without adventure, and she acquired the ease and facility of one who is at home in any situation. Although the two of them, mother and daughter, had in contrast to their friends hardly led a life of great luxury, it was none the less a life rich in experience and lived out on an international plane. To judge from photographs and pictures taken at the time, the young Countess Kinsky must have cut an elegant and beautiful figure, an attractive young lady who was also intelligent and had many accomplishments. Her education was better than the average and she was clearly destined to play a dominant role wherever she went.

So it was natural that such a fascinating personality should exercise a great attraction on other young people. Clearly the daughters of Baron Suttner were enthusiastic about their new governess and delighted to have about them someone who had seen so much of the "big world" and had got to know so many interesting people. It is understandable that the mutual attraction between the penniless countess—who was even now over thirty—and the younger son of the house, Arthur Gundaccar, seven years her junior, did not meet the full approval of his parents, even more so if one recalls that this romance was acted out in the seventies of the last century.

Once again in her life Countess Kinsky had to face up to the consequences of the situation in which she found herself; and so it was that in 1876 she made that remarkable and fateful journey to Paris, where she took up a position as secretary and house-keeper to a rich Swedish eccentric who went by the name of Alfred Nobel. Baroness Suttner had seen an advertisement in the *Neue Freie Presse*, and thought it would be a good idea to reply to it, and for the post to be accepted if a good offer was forth-coming. So the unhappy Bertha left the Suttners and made for Paris, where her grief at parting began to fade a little when she found herself having to converse with Nobel, whose later impor-tance she was scarcely able to guess at the time. In her memoirs she writes :

> Alfred Nobel's company helped to take me out of myself, for he was such an absorbing talker, storyteller, and philosopher that his conversation quite captivated the whole attention. It was a rare delight indeed to discuss with him the world and people, art and life, the problems of time and eternity.... About a week after my arrival Mr. Nobel had to make a brief trip to Sweden where a dynamite factory was being planned. The King himself had summoned him.[9]

And so it was that the interlude in Paris, which had lasted only a week, came to an end; so concluded the first meeting between the inventor of dynamite, who was ever seeking "to produce a substance or a machine which would be capable of such terrible mass destruction that war would be rendered utterly impos-sible",[10] and the woman who later sought to achieve the same objective through the power of the spoken and written word.

NOTES

1. Constant   Wurzbach,   *Biographisches   Lexikon   des   Kaisertums Österreich,* 1855–91.
2. *Memoiren,* Stuttgart, 1908, p. 15.
3. *Ibid.,* p. 62.
4. *Ibid.,* p. 63.
5. *High Life,* Dresden, 1886, p. 212.
6. *Memoiren,* p. 123.
7. Apart from official occasions, there was no difference in the form of address of "Freiherr" and "Baron".
8. *Memoiren,* p. 123f.
9. *Ibid.,* pp. 133–4.
10. *Ibid.,* p. 134.

MARRIAGE AND FLIGHT TO THE CAUCASUS

Shortly after Nobel's departure, she was overcome with homesickness, sold her last piece of jewellery and made her way back to Vienna. Here the lovers, meeting secretly—for Bertha's return could not be revealed to anyone—resolved never to be parted again; and in the parish church of St. Giles in Vienna-Gumpendorf (not Gumpoldskirchen; see the *Memoirs*) the marriage between Countess Bertha Kinsky and Arthur Gundaccar Baron Suttner took place in secret. Then the couple travelled, or rather fled, to Russia, to Princess von Mingrelia, a friend of the young bride from her Paris days. "From Vienna I had written to Dedopali (which means queen; literally, mother of mothers) and Prince Niko, who was resident in the Caucasus at the time, telling them the whole story and giving notice of our visit. They joyfully telegrammed 'Welcome' in reply."[1]

It is a pity Bertha Suttner destroyed her diaries for this period; still, her memoirs recapture the mood of that journey with great vividness. During the Black Sea crossing from Odessa to the harbour of Ponti both of them experienced "something resembling the spirit of the Argonauts, a blend of adventurousness, confidence in victory, a delirium of hope".[2]

Their travels which had begun in the "spirit of the Argonauts" were destined to last a long time : the Suttners remained in this part of Russia for nine years, cut off from any direct contact with European life and culture. Yet it was this period of her life that was to prove so crucial to her personal development.

It could not have been very easy for them at first : their joint income could hardly have been substantial, whether they were making up the complement of the prince's household in Gordi, or whether Baron Suttner was drawing up the plans for a castle for the son-in-law of Dedopali, a Murat, or indeed actually supervising the construction work, or again whether they were living in Tiflis or Zugdidi, the capital city—or rather "capital village"—of Mingrelia, giving private tuition or drawing up plans for a carpet factory. They lived the life of emigrants; and despite the favour of the countess they were obliged to rely completely on their own resources of skill and industry and their ingenuity in exploiting them to best advantage. After a day of unremitting toil they would don all their finery and pass the evening in the company of the local nobility.

They seem to have enjoyed this adventurous and hardworking mode of existence; in her book *Es Löwos*, Bertha Suttner sought to recapture the atmosphere of those days, and the two of them often reflected back on that time after they had returned to the narrow circle of family life in Austria, and they were more than happy to be able to go off on their travels again and spend a few months abroad.

Although they did not actually suffer poverty, Bertha does recall at one point in her memoirs that "on some days during that time we got to know the ghost of 'Hunger'"[3] and thus found themselves obliged to cast about for new and more profitable sources of income. Arthur Suttner was disappointed in his ambition to obtain a position at the court of the Czar despite the recommendation of the princess; when the war of 1877–78 between Russia and Turkey came, Arthur tried his hand at writing. Bertha recalls in her memoirs that

> his letters on the war, which were published in the press, were praised on many sides, and so it was that Arthur discovered his talent for writing in a relaxed, descriptive style.... Was it envy or the urge to imitate? I too wanted to see if I could make a go of writing. I had never really felt drawn to it.... I secretly composed a feuilleton called "Above and below Stairs" and sent it off to the Alte Press in Vienna.... and from then on I have continued to write, without interruption, up to the present day.[4]

At first Arthur Suttner wrote novels and short stories set in the Caucasus under the pseudonym of "A. G. Lerei". His work was assured a considerable success because of the exotic milieu, rendered more attractive through the Russo-Turkish war and the element of folklore, capped by a flowing, readable style and natural descriptions drawn from real experience. German publishers undertook to produce his works, periodicals were glad to print his short stories, among others the *Neue illustrierte Zeitung, Über Land und Meer*, and *Die Gartenlaube*. It was fiction-writing of a high order couched in the style of poetic realism. Later, after their return to Europe, he came under the influence of the early Naturalists and turned towards social themes and social criticism, as in *Eine moderne Ehe* and *Gebrandmarkt*. Arthur Suttner was also the founder of a league against anti-

Semitism; but for all that he remained in the shadow of his wife, who had now become the more famous of the two.

Bertha Suttner took up writing with her characteristic energy and vitality; at first she too published her works under a pseudonym, "B. Oulot", and later, for example in the case of the book *Age of the Machine*, under the name "Jemand" (Someone). But the Caucasus, its people and its landscape did not find their way into her works. She wrote in the main novels of social criticism or studies on a variety of questions of the day.

Neither of them had found the "golden fleece" in their Caucasus argosy, but there they had both embarked upon their work as writers. There they had been thrown back on their own resources and had made an intensive and serious study of the prevailing mood of distant Europe. When the fees began to come in and their standard of living was on the increase, they read all the books, newspapers and periodicals they were able to lay their hands on, in order to keep themselves informed on the intellectual and political situation in the world at large. "Among the authors whom we studied were Darwin, Haeckel, Herbert Spencer, Whewell, Carus, and Sterne. And one book above all others was a revelation to me : Buckle's *History of Civilisation*."[5] She fully accepted Darwin's theory of evolution, and H. T. Buckle's book was an important experience for her. Buckle had sought to relate the scientific theory of evolution to the investigation of history. It ought to be possible, he argues, to see man's past in terms of developmental laws and general historical principles.

Reading took up several hours of their daily programme, gave the impetus to discussion and debate, and so constituted the raw material which led the two of them on their return to Austria to embark upon their idealistic campaign against war and inhumanity and on behalf of peace for all mankind and a united Europe.

NOTES

1. *Memoiren,* p. 134.
2. *Ibid.,* p. 134.
3. *Ibid.,* p. 147.
4. *Ibid.,* p. 148.
5. *Ibid.,* p. 155.

FIRST STEPS AS A WRITER

The Suttners, now well known as writers and financially independent, came back to Austria in May 1885 after an absence of
nine years. They had proved that they could make their own
way in the world. There was a family reconciliation with these
fascinating two runaways. Since the parents had lost the major
part of their fortune in the years that Bertha and Arthur had
been away, the newly-returned couple found themselves obliged
to work on as hard as they could in order to preserve the family
from ruination. They had to write for several hours every day,
and the rest of the time was set aside for reading newspapers and
newly-published works in the field of literature and related
studies. They lived in the country with some members of the
family, the parents, three sisters and a niece, on the Harmannsdorf estate in Lower Austria. The grand palace in Vienna had
been sold. The Suttners were able to maintain their rhythm of
work away from the city, but in the years after their return they
also undertook considerable journeys and maintained contact
with other writers, especially with those who worked for the
Munich periodical *Die Gesellschaft*.[1]

Soon after the publication of her first works, and while she
was still in the Caucasus, Bertha Suttner had made contact with
the circle around M. G. Conrad, the leader of the Munich
"Moderne". In the very first issue of *Die Gesellschaft* her essay
"Truth and Falsehood", which was in the form of a dialogue, is
printed in pride of place. The choice of theme, form and style
are all typical of Bertha Suttner: she examines morality and
falsehood in a debate situation in polished language with many
turns of phrase borrowed from the salon conversation of the age,
for which one critic in the newspaper *Neue Freie Presse* casti-
gated her, claiming that her writing was "filled with stylistic
Achilles heels, oversights, slackness of expression, and that im-
precision of language which is—regrettably—so characteristic of
the conversation of high society".[2]

Die Gesellschaft was planned as a journal to campaign against
played-out "pseudo-art" and for the new, realistic art; it aspired
to be "a violent protest against any form of falsehood, whether

intended or not, in art and life, against any concealment or veiling of the truth".[3]—"We need a mouthpiece for completely unfettered humane sentiment, an unerring sense for truth, a resolutely realistic world-view."[4] These were the watchwords of the editor of this new periodical whose early days particularly are so important to an understanding of the beginnings of Naturalism. The writers in this group saw the new era and the new art in scientific terms. The task of creative literature was to hold up a mirror to the new scientific discoveries; man in literature is to be seen as subordinated to the laws of nature, for man too had been caught in the net of science; and the man of letters as the individual best endowed under this new scientific knowledge. The greatest and most revered model for this group around M. G. Conrad was Emile Zola whose stress upon truth "is the only motif—although it has not gained sufficient recognition as such—of eternal validity to emerge from Zola's theories and novels".[5]

Such revolutionary sentiments were in full accord with Bertha Suttner's views and personality; in her memoirs she writes with great admiration: "We followed all the stages of this revolution with the greatest interest. Conrad, Bleibtreu, Alberti—we read every word they wrote and were astonished at their audacity. Everywhere was in a ferment of activity."[6] On the occasion of a congress of the writers' club in Berlin in October 1885, in which Arthur and Bertha Suttner participated, they got to know some of these greatly admired authors personally. Bertha Suttner modelled herself upon them.

She assured herself the sympathy of her readers by campaigning on behalf of the causes she held to be right with passion but without prejudice. Thus in one of her first novels, *High Life*, she sings the praises of progress and democracy. The hero, a citizen of the United States, compares conditions abroad with those obtaining in his homeland. Bertha Suttner sees the new world as the land of the future. "The democratic spirit finds there neither thrones nor castles . . . and has therefore been able to develop its finest qualities to the full: namely, respect for the value of the individual and respect for work."[7] And she goes on: "Today we are still content to do no more than provide the economically underprivileged parts of the world with corn, dried meat, sewing machines and electric lamps, but the day may yet come when we shall send them spiritual light and nourishment too."[8]

In *A Bad Lot*, a much-travelled, still youngish man returns to the home of his conservative family and openly expresses his modern views: ". . . the old spirit or the new? No question about it, I value the new, a thousand times more highly!" Or again: "My favourite hero is Stanley, who opened a new area of the world to development, and my favourite political system the constitutional." And further: "International politics? Free trade! . . . The question of women? Equal rights! . . . In matters of love? Freedom for the heart! . . . In matters of religion? Freedom of thought! . . . In matters of war? Guaranteed peace!"[9]

Problems like Darwinism and anti-Semitism, which were burning issues of the day, find frequent cause for discussion in the novel *Daniela Dormes*. The heroine, a rich widow, falls in love with an educated, but impecunious Jewish scholar who gives her lessons in philosophy. This provides an opportunity for the discussion of books like Renan's *Life of Christ*, of Darwin and his theories, of anti-Semitism, and much more besides. Darwin is revered without reservation:

> If there were an orthodox cult of Darwin, I should wish to be its High Priest. I adulate this man whose untiring pursuit of knowledge and ability to think a problem through to its end have laid the foundations for a new concept of life which will mark the greatest turning-point yet in the history of man's development.[10]

One of the principal themes of the novel *Before the Storm* is socialism. Three friends, a dreamer who wants to found a "society for ethical culture", an active social democrat and a Baltic German who has fled from Russia, all discuss their plans for the future. The fantasy of the first man is one of purifying all "elements of society", to which the social democrat replies:

> I have every admiration for your aspirations, my friend. But we are involved in a world of practicalities. And—without knowing it—so are you. "Do not ignore the social question?" That is hardly a generous gesture. No one ignores it any more. But not because it is a question, but rather because it is regarded either as a threat or a promising prospect—depending on your views. If democratic socialism existed only in theory, consisting of impractical notions and pamphleteering, then you could either discard it scornfully, indifferently, leaving it uncomprehended, or you could carry on writing pamphlets about its impracticality. But social democrats exist. They are living beings; there is a substantial party, organised, disciplined, widespread, growing daily—having funds at its disposal, proclaiming its existence

by act and deed, in strikes, May Day celebrations and congresses; the armies of workers stand ready, they are not yet actually on the march, but people think they can hear the sound of their advancing feet—so you can't ignore the question any more.... What the progressive and democratic parties are severally striving towards, fundamental principles which the most varied societies, parties and groups have come together to realise : these things already form part of our programme and, more than that, some of them have actually been carried through as a result of our initiative. Women's societies campaign for the right of women to earn—the female worker is already among our ranks, and when we demand universal suffrage, we naturally demand it for both sexes; we have sought to unite all nations in peace by forming a union which cuts across political frontiers and diplomatic considerations; our party programme bears the slogan : "War is done away with!" National alliances are combatting one nation's encroachment on or suppression of another; we will have no truck with racial hatred nor with national pride, we utterly reject aggression and stand firm against enslavement. School groups and societies for the advancement of art and science are striving to achieve the spread of education and to lead the people to the treasure chest of knowledge and the pleasures of art; we demand their benefits as of right, and want to create opportunities for exploiting this right, for subsistence wages and thirteen hours' work a day do not go hand in hand with education. We want bread, but we also want leisure.

The Russian revolutionary replies to this enthusiastic speech; he has made it his task to undertake a study of democratic socialism in all countries of the world.

I wish to put to you the objections I have to raise against social democrat doctrines. They threaten the rights of the individual. They are a form of tyranny : the unrestricted dictatorship of the majority. The sins of the state : forceful maintenance of monopolies, privileges, exploitation of work, subjection of the individual will—these are the things the majority are now supposed to take over. At present a minority terrorises and violates the masses—but what will happen when the masses violate the minority? What will come about when individual initiative is prohibited by society, and the hope of profit which acts as a spur to work is replaced by the compulsion to work? —For this will turn men into robots, cause the mainsprings of initiative to rust away and thus paralyse the principal factor in human progress. Personal freedom! Do you not see how greatly this priceless treasure will be damaged by your "socialist" doctrines?...After the nationalisation of all the means of production and the institution of the planned economy, then the spirit of personal freedom will rise up in revolt against this regimentation of the spirit. The individual will not permit himself to be dehumanised.[11]

Each of her books, then, devotes itself to specific themes which were preoccupying their authoress at the time, and which were also the object of discussion in the journals and the daily press. She is not concerned with man the individual, his soul, his personality or his fate; she instead devotes her attention to problems which she examines from a variety of angles and which relate to mankind as a whole. None of the figures in these novels, despite attempts at individualisation, is much more than a colourless type who proclaims the views of his authoress with varying degrees of pedantry. The principal protagonist represents the principal theme; the others utter the appropriate slogans. One of her critics observes that in her works thought drives out observation and emotion.[12] But she was so captivated by the parry and thrust of theories, ideas, and ideals that she herself admits:

> I am a great admirer of the *roman à these*. The reason why ... I am so taken up by this kind of novel is that it is based on a quality which in my eyes sets it above all other forms of fictional writing. And that is the ability to give the reader an opportunity to decide for or against the views advanced and thereby activate his own powers of thought, creating in him a delight in debate and the interaction of ideas, from which a few sparks of truth must surely emerge.[13]

To scan the long list of titles of her works, many of which appeared as short stories in lesser-known journals and have now all but been forgotten, one would gain the impression that she worked with great speed and facility. Although, as she herself said, she did not feel within herself the "vocation" of a writer, but began writing out of an urge to imitate, to compete with her husband, her delight in communicating her own thoughts and the success that attended her efforts must have encouraged her to continue writing, all the more so because the fees she received, even in the days before *Lay Down Your Arms*, were not meagre by any standards.

Her earnings supplemented their income and allowed the couple to make longish stays abroad; so it was that in 1886–87 they were in Paris, where they again met Alfred Nobel and other people she knew from her youth in Paris as well as new acquaintances from the Caucasus. But the Suttners also made contact with the writers of the French capital and became involved in the general social life of the city.

It was Nobel who gave the Suttners an entrée into the house of the writer Juliette Adam, the editor of the *Nouvelle Revue*, in whose literary and political salon the main topic of conversation in the winter of 1886–87 was the tension between France and Germany. The lively discussions which took place caused Bertha Suttner to ask herself how it was that a woman could become so intensely involved with political issues. "How much unpleasantness and even ridicule she has to endure! And how on earth can she also burden herself with editing a review!"[14]

She also met members of the Académie Française and the editorial staff of the *Revue des deux Mondes* in the house of its editor, Charles Buloz, one of the centres of literary and intellectual life in Paris at that time. Her circle of acquaintances also included the journalist Max Nordau, Ernest Renan, Victor Cherbuliez, Ludovic Halévy, and Alphonse Daudet.

NOTES

1. The full title is *Die Gesellschaft, realistische Wochenschrift für Literatur, Kunst und öffentliches Leben* (Society, a Weekly Journal for Literature, the Arts and Public Affairs).
2. *Neue Freie Presse*, 9 June 1893 (H. Glücksmann).
3. A. Soergel, *Dichtung und Dichter der Zeit*, Leipzig, 1916, p. 31.
4. *Die Gesellschaft*, no. 1, 1 January 1885.
5. A. Soergel, *Dichtung und Dichter der Zeit*, Leipzig, 1916, p. 82.
6. *Memorien*, p. 165.
7. *High Life*, Dresden, 1886, p. 125.
8. *Ibid.*, p. 125f.
9. *Ein schlechter Mensch*, Dresden, 1885, p. 291f.
10. *Daniela Dormes*, Dresden, 1886, p. 114.
11. *Vor dem Gewitter*, Dresden, 1893, p. 142ff.
12. *Neu Freie Presse*, 9 June 1893 (H. Glücksmann).
13. *Doktor Hellmuts Donnerstage. Vom Buchstaben zum Geiste*, Dresden, 1892, p. 49f.
14. *Memoiren*, p. 172.

INTERNATIONAL ARBITRATION AND PEACE ASSOCIATION

As she records in her memoirs, Bertha Suttner discovered in Paris,

> in the course of a conversation on war and peace (an issue which even at that time preoccupied me greatly), that there existed in London an "International Arbitration and Peace Association" whose objective it was to mobilise public opinion in order to achieve the establishment of an international court which would replace armed combat as a means of settling disputes between nations.... This information electrified me.... On my return I found the proofs of my book *The Age of the Machine*. To my chapter "Prospects for the Future" I added a report on the London Association.[1]

This International Arbitration and Peace Association had been founded in 1880 by Hodgson Pratt. It differed from the other peace societies existing in London at the time—for example, the Peace Society established in 1816, which was more religious in character, or the International Arbitration League, instituted by Randall W. Cremer in 1868, which mainly sought to interest the working population in the idea of peace—in that it was specifically political in character. It was the object of its founder to set up societies on the London model in every country, or in as many countries as possible, and then to bring them all together in one huge confederation. Hodgson Pratt travelled Europe in the eighties, visiting the continental capitals, where he held public lectures on the purpose and objectives of his International Peace Association which was in the early years of its existence. He succeeded in gaining supporters and friends and in setting up several branches of his Association.

What were the goals of the peace movement at the time when Bertha Suttner became aware of it in Paris, the movement which was to change the rest of her life and alter its character so profoundly? Not unnaturally, the principal objective was to put an end to war. But a fundamental distinction was drawn between war and a struggle for existence. In nature, conflict takes on as many forms as life itself, say the pacifists; it is conditioned by nature and finds its expression in human community life in the form of healthy competition.

But war, of the kind which man has waged hitherto by force of arms, is the one specific manifestation of this struggle for existence which must be stopped, which must be rendered impossible.

Peace, as it was generally conceived at the time, was nothing more than a state of armistice between one war and the next. But peace of the kind the pacifists were striving to bring to the world was only to be achieved if the civilised nations were prepared to take common interests as the basis for harmonious co-existence. An open treaty system among the nations must be instituted which would exclude the use of force, and justice and reciprocity must predominate. If, despite this, disputes arise between individual states, they should be judged by standard legal procedures and settled on this basis by an international tribunal.

As soon as such a union of justice were founded and had proved itself, disarmament would be a natural consequence, and would take place automatically in all states at the same time. Even before such a union is set up it should be possible to achieve limitation or even a ban on new armaments, in the first instance during a limited period of time only.

An international arbitration tribunal would be the "crowning glory" of such a system and would be a living demonstration of the victory of justice over force of arms. A standing treaty of justice would be no more than a logical consequence of such developments.

So the concrete objectives of the peace movement were an international league, arbitration and disarmament through which mankind might hope to attain and secure peace for the future.

NOTE

1. *Memoiren,* p. 176f.

"LAY DOWN YOUR ARMS"

Bertha Suttner was an enthusiastic supporter of the ideas of the International Arbitration and Peace Association, and she resolved to do "some service" for them. This took the form of writing a book, a novel, which told the story of a woman who lived through the wars of 1859, 1864, 1866 and 1870–71 and who suffered greatly as a consequence. Such is the origin of *Lay down your Arms*. In this novel, Martha von Tilling tells the story of her life, beginning with the brief happiness of her first marriage which ended with the death of her first husband on the battlefield at Magenta in 1859. She tells of her second husband's participation in the Austrian campaign in Schleswig-Holstein against the Danes in 1864 and the Austro-Prussian war in Bohemia in 1866, in which he is wounded. As she receives no news of him for a long time, she goes to look for him herself on the battlefield of Königgrätz. There she witnesses the unimaginable sufferings of the wounded, most of whom are destined to die a terrible death in agony with no adequate medical treatment. The cholera epidemic, which breaks out in Austria after the war, takes her closest relations from her. After a few short years of peace, in which she and her husband, both horrified at the terrible experiences of their recent past, become acquainted with the efforts of the peace movement, the couple are caught in Paris at the outbreak of war in 1870. As Austrians, they are not directly involved, and so remain in the French capital, but they are not able to leave before the siege of Paris by German forces; her husband, Colonel Tilling retired, is taken for a spy by an angry mob, "dragged before a tribunal of patriots, and on 1 February 1871, shot by order of a court-martial".[1]

A succession of publishers and editors of periodicals returned the manuscript to Bertha Suttner. Her own publisher Pierson of Dresden was not particularly impressed and insisted that if the manuscript were to be published there should be several changes and cuts. "For me the risk is considerable, because the novel's substantial length would cause high printing and distribution costs."[2] Pierson did not think it likely that any journal would reprint the novel. But Bertha Suttner managed to overcome his reservations. The novel appeared under the title she herself had chosen, without any cuts or alterations, and became a world-wide sensation. It was epoch-making in a way that perhaps only one other novel has been, Harriet Beecher-Stowe's *Uncle Tom's Cabin*.

Later generations have not always found it easy to understand why a particular book becomes a best-seller when it first comes out. *Lay down your Arms*, from a literary point of view, is by no means a greater work than her earlier novels, and it is certainly no masterpiece. Its topicality of theme does not mark it out from her other works, because they too are topical. *Lay down your Arms* owes its enormous impact primarily to the considerable contemporary interest in the issue of "maintaining the peace", which was engaging the attention of substantial numbers of people at that time, not only in Europe but elsewhere, especially in the United States. But due credit should also go to Bertha Suttner's courage—which evoked universal admiration—in writing in this form and from this particular point of view, namely that of the suffering woman, about the brutality of war, its effects and consequences. Like Zola before her, as she herself records, she researched her subject thoroughly to produce descriptions of milieu as close as possible to the original.

None of her later books had anything approaching the success of *Lay down your Arms*, not even its sequel, which appeared in 1902 under the title *Martha's Children*. It was a unique stroke of fortune for her that she was able to create a novel on this theme in a universally comprehensible manner at the right historical moment.

After she had become actively involved in the work of the international peace movement there was never enough time or leisure for her to be able to devote all her energies to her writing. Later in life she was often to complain in her diaries about a lack of imagination and a falling-off in her creative powers. These she regarded as signs of approaching old age. In reality, she was so totally committed to her work for the peace movement that she could no longer find the time to concentrate on writing a novel, although she did continue her journalistic activities. She did not possess sufficient flexibility of mind to adapt herself to the style of the age, the style of the modern novelist.

The first edition of her novel *Lay down your Arms* was published at the end of 1889 in an edition of one thousand copies, for which she received an honorarium of 1,000 Marks, in two instalments of 500 Marks each, the first instalment to be paid when printing was completed, the second after the end of the 1890 Leipzig book fair. This edition quickly sold out. In a note of 4 March 1890 E. Pierson was already observing: "I am now quite confident about *Lay down your Arms*." And as early as 16 June he was writing with a sense of urgency: "We must have a second impression out as quickly as possible." On 18 July of the same year he stated: "I agree with your proposal to print the second and third thousand right away." And on 28 of September he reports: "We have received a flood of orders for the new edition of *Lay down your Arms*."[3] Bertha Suttner received 1,000 Marks for each of the first three printings, for the fourth and subsequent impressions only 750 Marks each, but for the popular edition of 1896 (first to eighth thousand) 2,000 Marks. In 1905, when Bertha Suttner was awarded the Nobel Prize, the number of editions and impressions had already reached thirty-seven. And above and beyond this, the book had been translated into virtually every European language.

The name "Bertha von Suttner" had become associated with a revolt against the old order of things in which war was regarded as an inevitable phenomenon in the history of the nations. A confession of faith in peace and the portrayal of war in all its horror, the unmasking of the hollow pathos with which valour and heroism were adulated, long before the poets of Expressionism undertook the same task more crudely and brutally during and after the First World War, marked an act of real courage at a time when vast sums were already being poured into rearmament and all possible means of propaganda were being exploited towards the glorification of war. Nor was it too difficult in those days to stir up the enthusiasm of the masses for war, since the generation of 1900 or so, in contrast to the present generation, had no knowledge of the terrible destruction of global war, nor had they any notion of "total war", let alone atomic war.

Enthusiasm for this novel on the part of some critics was countered by outrage at her "dishonouring" of true heroism. Bertha Suttner collected huge numbers of newspaper articles and letters and carefully preserved them, whether they were in favour of her book or against it. Among her papers after her death along with all the others no less than 157 anonymous letters were found which had been written to her on the subject of *Lay down your Arms*.

The Austrian philosopher and parliamentary delegate B. Carneri wrote about the book in the *Neue Freie Presse* on 15 March 1890, where he states:

Why does the name of the author and not the title of the book stand at the head of these lines? Because *Lay down your Arms* is an undying memorial to her. In its pages, she takes up her stand against the trends of the age with true heroism and declares war on war. Never before has militarism been so ruthlessly exposed for the suffering it causes, never before have we been shown how sweet the life can be which the militarist scorns. Her clear-headed logic remorselessly demonstrates how the most insignificant of causes can lead to the most terrifying results whose ultimate and inevitable consequence is war; how the smallest stone which any child could lift with ease can be set in motion and cause an avalanche destroying all in its path.

Carneri is full of praise for the work:

In the novel before us we find a kind of Naturalism such as true art demands, not the negation of idealism but the ideal clothed in living flesh. We are not just told how people ought to be; we are shown men as they could be. It is a book which in the truest sense of the word is ennobling, for it reveals to us the full magic of genuine love, and also its undying value.... For all the courage with which the truth is here made plain to all, there are some things in the novel which by usual standards might not be fully admissible. But it is this very courage which has filled us with admiration, and the acolytes of militarism are so numerous today and from among their ranks such embittered opponents of the book have appeared, that we can safely leave it to them to point out any little defects there may be.... The more who read it, the greater will be the number of those who will set it down with the cry "Lay down your arms!"

Her old acquaintance, Alfred Nobel, congratulated her on her courageous campaign in a charming letter:

Dear Baroness and friend,

I have just finished reading your admirable masterpiece. It is said that there are 2,000 languages—1,999 too many—but there is not a single language into which your excellent work should not be translated, and then read and dwelt upon.

How long did it take you to create such a marvel? You will tell me when I have the honour and good fortune to shake you by the hand—the hand of an Amazon so bravely declaring war upon war itself.

It is not really right of you to declare : "Lay down your arms", because you make use of weapons yourself, and your weapons— the charm of your style and the nobility of your ideas—have a far greater range than the hellish weapons of war.

Yours ever

Paris, 1 April 1890   A Nobel.

In a debate in the imperial council on the military budget (18 April 1891) Finance Minister Julian Ritter von Dunajevski said the following : "A book has recently appeared entitled *Lay down your Arms*—I can do no other than invite you, sirs, to devote a few hours to perusing this novel; and I can but pity anyone who then still feels any love for war."[5]

The Russian writer Leo Tolstoy addressed these words of admiration to her :

Dear Madam,

I was just reading your novel *Lay down your Arms*, which H. Boulgakoff had sent me, when I received your letter. I esteem your work highly, and it has occurred to me that the publication of your novel represents a good omen for the future.

The abolition of slavery was preceded by a famous novel written by a woman, H. Beecher-Stowe. May God grant that the abolition of war will follow on your novel. I do not believe that arbitration is an effective enough means towards the abolition of war. I am just finishing a paper on this very subject, in which I discuss what is in my opinion the sole means of rendering war impossible. All endeavours founded upon a true love of humanity will bear fruit and the congress of Rome will, I am utterly convinced, like the one in London last year, contribute a great deal to make the public at large understand the all too familiar state of conflict in which Europe finds itself, the military state of the nations, and the Christian and human principles which they embrace.

Permit me, Madam, to express to you my sincere respect and sympathy.

10/12 October 1891   Leo Tolstoy[6]

The Austrian writer Peter Rosegger, who valued Bertha Suttner's endeavours highly and supported them, wrote in a letter to her on 9 October 1891 with great enthusiasm : "This book is a real achievement ! Reading it was a landmark in my life",[7] and in the November issue of his journal *Der Heimgarten* for 1891 published a detailed discussion of the novel, part of which runs as follows :

During the quiet autumn days of this year I sat down in the woodland near Krieglach and read the book *Lay down your Arms* by Bertha von Suttner. I took two days to read it, and these two days represent a landmark in my life. When I finished reading it, I was filled with the strong desire to see this book translated into every civilised tongue, sold in every single bookshop and introduced into every school. There are societies for propagating the Bible, and there ought to be a society for spreading knowledge of this remarkable book, which I am more than tempted to call an epoch-making work.[8]

Newspapers of the widest variety of political complexions were eager to reprint the novel in their pages, for example, the *Stuttgarter Beobachter*, or even a children's newspaper, and in 1892 the editor-in-chief of *Vorwärts* approached Bertha Suttner with a view to printing *Lay down your Arms* in his paper. She concurred, waiving the fee of 300 Marks she was offered: "The party which makes international peace the main point of its programme is the one best fitted to giving this book a sympathetic reception, and will in this spirit perhaps extend the same sympathy to the peace league which pursues the identical objective—international justice—as the *sole* point in its programme."[9] Liebknecht thanked her in these words: " . . . and you will find your reward in the growing seed which you have sown. What you aspire towards, namely, peace on earth, we shall carry through. By 'we' I mean democratic socialism, which is in truth itself a great international peace league."[10]

As late as 1913 a film company was still expressing interest in turning the novel into a film, and Bertha Suttner was approached with a view to her writing a scenario. The film was produced, and photographs of the authoress were to have been made as introductory material. In the programme for the peace congress planned for Vienna in September 1914 the following is included: "17 September 1914. Film performance in the Beethoven hall; in honour of the congress the première of the film *Lay down your Arms* after the novel of the same name by Baroness von Suttner, filmed by the Nordisk Film Co. in Copenhagen."[11]

Her enemies attacked her viciously and cruelly and often made fun at the expense of her tireless campaigning,[12] and Bertha Suttner suddenly found herself in the midst of a violent controversy. People took extreme stands for or against; support for or opposition to *Lay down your Arms* amounted to a confession of political faith, implied commitment in a conflict of embattled philosophies.

Many years later, after all the agitation had died away, Bertha Suttner—still clearly amazed at the unexpected furore—wrote in her memoirs :

> I had composed the book in order to render in my own way a service to the peace movement, of whose growing organisation I had heard—and the contacts and experiences I gained as a result of the book caused me to become more and more caught up in the movement, so much so that in the end I was not just working for the cause with my pen, as I had originally intended, but with my whole being.[13]

In Paris in 1886 Bertha Suttner had made her first fateful contact with the International Arbitration and Peace Association, and thus with the international peace movement at large; this was followed at the end of 1889 by the publication of the novel *Lay down your Arms* and its sensational success. Both events were paving the way to her subsequent political activity, which only really began as a result of the experiences and meetings which took place during her stay in Venice in the winter of 1890–91.

NOTES

1. *Die Waffen nieder! Eine Lebensgeschichte*, Dresden, 1892, 2 vols., p. 295.
2. Library of the United Nations, Geneva, Peace archives, collection Suttner-Fried. Letter from E. Pierson to B. von Suttner dated 28 January 1889 (Ir 1–65).
3. Collection Suttner-Fried (Ir 1–65).
4. *Ibid.* Letter from A. Nobel to B. von Suttner dated 1 April 1890 (Du 9).
5. *Memoiren*, p. 183.
6. Collection Suttner-Fried (Du 9).
7. *Ibid.* (Dq 4).
8. *Der Heimgarten*, 1891.
9. *Vorwärts*, Berlin, 20 August 1892.
10. Collection Suttner-Fried (Fd 6a).
11. *Memoiren*, p. 183.
12. It was in this spirit that Felix Dahn composed these lines, which are not in the best of taste, which reflect the role reversal implicit in a woman's action in taking up the cudgels in a male province :
    Die Waffen hoch! Das Schwert ist Mannes eigen,
    Wo Männer fechten, hat das Weib zu schweigen,
    Doch freilich, Männer gibt's in diesen Tagen,
    die sollten lieber Unterröcke tragen.
    (*Ibid.*, p. 183.)
13. *Ibid.*, p. 183f.

FIRST YEARS OF THE INTERPARLIAMENTARY UNION

The Suttners decided not to remain in Harmannsdorf any longer; this was probably the result of the success of Bertha Suttner's novel, which had brought her in considerable sums of money. In autumn 1890 they rented the Palazzo Dario on the Grand Canal in Venice, and spent the winter of 1890–91 there. The Austrian consul, Baron Krauss, introduced them to local society. In Venice they also met acquaintances and friends from Georgia and Italy, among them Marchese Pandolfi who had married an Austrian girl, a friend from Bertha Suttner's youth. The Marchese, who was Sicilian delegate in the Italian house of representatives, numbered among those parliamentarians who had taken the initiative in forming a group to represent Italy at the interparliamentary conferences which had been held since 1888.

In Venice she also met a member of the committee of the London International Arbitration and Peace Association, Felix Moscheles, a painter and writer by occupation. He came originally from Leipzig, where his father, a famous musician and friend of Felix Mendelssohn-Bartholdy, worked for many years at the conservatory. Felix Moscheles told her more about the membership and activities of the Association. The Bishop of London, together with representatives of the nobility, for example the Duke of Westminster and Lord Ripon, were members of the committee. Its composition was characteristic of the various groups that made up the peace movement which in the years before 1914 did not undergo any real fundamental changes. One might find prominent men of religion, aristocrats, Jews, always some idealists, but no card-carrying members of left-wing parties. Only in the early days were active politicians members of the individual peace societies; they subsequently directed their attention towards the work of other international organisations, in particular the interparliamentary conferences, whose area of activity coincided with their own political operations.

In the Palazza Dario, the Suttner residence in Venice, Marchese Pandolfi, a politician given to enthusiasm, met Felix

Moscheles, the artist and idealist. It was resolved to form a peace society in Venice on the model of H. Pratt's association. An ad hoc committee was set up, notices published, and a meeting fixed. There was sufficient interest aroused, and so the meeting duly took place; Pandolfi gave a fiery speech in which he exhorted those present to form a Venetian branch of the peace movement, nor did he neglect as a parliamentarian to expound the goals of the interparliamentary groups. In this way Bertha Suttner received her instructions in the technique of forming an association.

In those days there was still a considerable measure of co-operation between the participants in the interparliamentary conferences (the name Interparliamentary Union did not gain currency until around 1900) and members of the international peace movement. This was largely so because the meetings between parliamentarians came about mainly as a result of initiatives by members of the peace movement. The historian Professor Ludwig Quidde pointed out in a study of the beginnings of the Interparliamentary Union that

> the more organised the peace movement became, the more it concerned itself with effective practical politics and the more it attracted the attention of parliaments, the greater attention was given to the notion of bringing together the parliamentarians of the various countries, because it is they who were in the very best position to exert pressure on the policies of their governments and because too the problems which lay before them clearly demanded international co-operation.[1]

In this context it is not inappropriate to recall that the very first man to point to the need for a closer degree of co-operation among the parliamentarians of all countries was an Austrian, Robert von Walterskirchen, in a speech given on 27 August 1870. Another Austrian politician, Adolf Fischhof, caused something of a stir in 1875 in an article on the reduction of the continental armies; at the beginning of 1876 he demanded in the house of representatives "the holding of a European conference of parliamentary delegates". On 27 April 1876 a gathering of Austrian parliamentarians took place which resolved to send a delegation to the conference of representatives of all parliaments planned by the Spanish senator Artur de Marcoartu. Fischhof also entered into correspondence with the secretary of the London Peace Society, Henry Richard, and won over the support of French and Italian deputies to the idea of yearly conferences. Their main theme was to be arbitration, but Fisch-hof himself placed the principal emphasis upon the limitation of arms. Despite this decision no one in Austria seems to have taken advantage of the opportunity, and as a result no Austrian parliamentarian actively worked towards or was represented at the preliminary discussions or at the first parliamentary conferences.

The first meeting of parliamentarians, the supporters of this novel idea, took place in Paris in 1888, where Frédéric Passy, who was a deputy of the French parliament in addition to being the founder of the Sociéte française des Amis de la Paix, joined Randall W. Cremer in leading discussions with French parliamentarians. The first session took place on 31 October 1888, with only French and English representatives taking part. The first interparliamentary conference on a truly international scale was held in Paris in June of the following year. Attendance was sparse, but there were enough present for a permanent institution to be founded. A committee was formed, composed of eight French and an equal number of English representatives, three Italians and three from Hungary. The second conference met in London in 1890; here the numbers had already grown to 111 representatives from eleven parliaments. One of its decisions was the formation of international committees in every country.

Marchese Pandolfi had naturally told Bertha Suttner and her husband all about the aspirations and objectives of this interparliamentary group, to which he himself belonged. In her memoirs, Bertha Suttner records—and there is no cause to doubt the truth of her words—that on her return to Vienna she related with great enthusiasm but no real understanding what the Marchese had told her to a circle of her friends which met regularly in the Hotel Meissl and Schadn in the New Market in Vienna, and to which Carneri and other parliamentarians also belonged. "The gentlemen listened with interest, but with most sceptical expressions on their faces. Not one of them thought of joining the movement."[2] From Pandolfi she received further news of his successes in the Italian chamber; 300 senators and deputies had formally expressed support, and it was his great ambition to see Austria join those nations represented in the 1891 conference which was scheduled to take place in Rome.

There is no doubt that Bertha Suttner energetically employed her connexions with various Austrian politicians in an attempt to win them over to the idea of international co-operation among parliamentarians. In her memoirs, she published some of the replies she received to her letters, all couched in the politest but most cautious of terms. It was not only politicians of the right, like Baron Max Kübeck, who reacted with extreme caution but also the socialist deputy E. Pernerstorfer, or the President of the museum of industrial technology, Dr. W. Exner. She goes on to state that federal council deputy Baron Pirquet was particularly interested; and it was his initiative that made it possible to bring together a group of parliamentarians. So Austria was represented after all in the 1891 Rome conference.

The national council archives in Vienna unfortunately contain only a small amount of material on the beginnings of the inter-parliamentary conferences; and it is not clear whether the caution on the part of the politicians was a result of lack of interest in the project or extreme caution in the face of Bertha Suttner's excessive zeal. For, according to documents in the archives, the deputies who officially declared their interest in participating in the 1891 conference included Dr. W. Exner, Baron Kübeck and E. Pernerstorfer. Marchese Pandolfi was also in correspondence with the President of the chamber of deputies, Dr. Franz Smolka. A letter has been preserved which contains the following:

Dear Mr. President,

We owe it solely to your esteemed interest that up until the present time 26 members of the chamber of deputies have promised to attend. It would be a particular pleasure for me if a large Austrian contingent came to Rome, firstly because I have the greatest feelings of friendship towards your country, since I have married an Austrian myself, and secondly, because I think that the most appropriate location for the next conference might well be Vienna.[3]

NOTES

1. *Die Interparlamentarische Union von 1889–1939,* Lausanne, 1939, p. 3.
2. *Memoiren,* p. 197.
3. Archives of the Austrian parliament, Austrian Federal Council (house of deputies) IB Präsidium, letter of 9 September 1891.

FOUNDATION OF THE AUSTRIAN PEACE SOCIETY
AND THE ROME CONGRESS 1891

The Marchese's letters had served to intensify the Suttners' interest in the interparliamentary conferences and the international peace movement in general. They were filled with a desire to join the struggle for common ideas and ideals, to be present themselves in Rome and to gain personal contact with the well-known figures in the peace movement, all the more so since the "peace congress", that is, the congress of the "private peace societies", was also taking place in Rome at about the same time. The congresses had been held on an annual basis since 1889 and continued to take place in subsequent years under the title of world peace congress. The congress arranged to take place between 11 and 14 November 1891 in Rome was the third of the series, and the number of those taking part rendered it by far the most important. Its sessions were due to be held in the rooms of the Palazzo del Senatore on the Capitol, and the representatives of the individual states were first to be welcomed by leading civic and government dignitaries. It was Bertha Suttner's burning desire to see Austria join those nations represented at this congress. She displayed remarkable energy to this end. On 3 September 1891 the readers of the *Neue Freie Presse* were invited to participate in the formation of an Austrian Society for the Friends of Peace. The response was unexpectedly large. Considerable numbers of people sought membership, financial donations flooded in, a meeting took place to constitute the society at which Bertha Suttner was elected lady president, and so she herself was actually able to participate in the congress of the international peace movement in Rome.

"It all happened so quickly," she remarked in her memoirs:

> I had acted under the influence of such an irresistible impulse, under the spell of such a burning desire but at the same time in the bliss of that kind of ignorance which is born of unawareness of the difficulties and obstacles in my path and which is a far better guide in any bold venture than experience and mature consideration.

When we arrived, the interparliamentary conference was still in full swing : our own congress was not due to begin until two days later. Practically all the participants in the two gatherings had booked into the Hotel Quirinal. So it was that the entire international community of pacifists (although the word "pacifism" had not been coined at the time) came into direct and continual personal contact, in the big restaurant at meal-times, in the public rooms and discussion groups, in the salons conversing together. Here I found all my old friends and colleagues, everyone I had long been in correspondence with, and many new friends besides.[1]

Bertha Suttner was most enthusiastic at the organisation of the congress, she felt greatly honoured, and at the opening session on the Capitol she gave her first big public speech.

Quite calmly, dispassionately, and with buoyant spirits, I said what I had to say, and my words were greeted by a torrent of applause. . . . I had something to say which to me seemed important, and which I knew would be welcome tidings to those of like mind who were all about me. . . and for this reason I spoke quite without fear, and with the confidence of a messenger who has clear and joyous tidings to convey.[2]

Her confidence and lack of inhibition are gifts that appear to have remained with her through the years; they permitted her, on her lecture tours of Europe and later in the United States, to gain effortless contact with her hearers on every occasion.

NOTES

1. *Memoirs*, p. 220.
2. *Ibid.*, p. 225.

A CAREER AS POLITICIAN AND JOURNALIST
BEGINS

Her experience of the world peace congress in Rome and her decision to work actively in the future for the international peace movement gave a new, positive direction to her life and her work. Up until this time she had been a freelance writer, but now as president of a society she took upon herself all the manifold tasks and problems which by the very nature of things constitute the burdens of office : disappointments, annoyances, but also valuable friendships, international contacts and travels. The years that followed were a continuous round of conferences and resolutions, and she was utterly absorbed in her new area of activity.

In her memoirs, which are essential to any study of Bertha Suttner, she describes with great vividness how greatly she was encouraged by her new friends and supporters to devote "her whole person" to the cause of peace. In her writings she names a great number of personalities who stood in close contact with one another like members of some masonic brotherhood. Congresses were held, countless letters changed hands, political activities went on both behind closed doors and in the full public glare. Constant attempts were being made to exercise personal influence upon rulers and ministers, articles were published in international organs or their own journals, there was unceasing pressure, criticism and effort directed towards shifting the pattern of events into the directions advocated by the peace movement. Relations between the members of the peace movement spread like an invisible web from Czarist Russia, across Europe and even stretched out as far as the United States.

The Suttners too were caught up in this web, willing prisoners who regarded it as their duty to serve the ideals of this international community. Bertha Suttner became one of the most prominent representatives of the international peace movement and was universally known as the "lady president" of the Austrian Peace Society. She was famed as a writer both home and abroad, but above all as the authoress of the novel *Lay down your Arms*, and well-known in international society as a member of the Austrian aristocracy; both at court and in society at large she succeeded in spreading her ideals, for which she was prepared to sacrifice her entire life, and in popularising them to such an extent that she was able to exercise a considerable influence upon all levels of the population. Like a perfect gentleman, Alfred Suttner kept in the background, but gave the fullest support to her endeavours.

In Austria the peace movement, as contemporary sources demonstrate, undeniably owes almost its entire great forward impetus to the efforts of Bertha Suttner. Even the membership of the leadership of the Austrian Peace Society in 1893 is significant in this respect, as can be seen from a report on a meeting of the Vienna Society:

> At the chairman's table: Bertha von Suttner; Prince Wrede; A. v. Czyzek (chief of the Czyzek banking concern); Hans von Czyzek; Alexander Fischel, local councillor for Frauenberg; H. Fürst, editor of the *Neues Wiener Tagblatt;* Balduin Groller; Freiherr v. Hackelberg, federal council deputy; Leopold Katscher; Freiherr v. Krafft-Ebing, university professor; Dr. Kunwald, court advocate; Freiherr v. Pirquet, federal council deputy; Freiherr A. G. v. Suttner.
>
> Apologies: Rudolf Count Hoyos; Duke v. Oldenburg; P. K. Rosegger; Prince Starhemberg, member of the royal house.[1]

The government and the civil service also lent their support to the friends of peace. The association of Austrian civil servants, which at that time numbered around 50,000 members, joined the Peace Society in 1906, in order to advance a social cause and "because a reduction in armaments, which will be an inevitable consequence of the policies of the peace societies, cannot help but improve the material lot of the civil servant".[2]

As president of the Vienna Peace Society, Bertha Suttner undertook many arduous tasks, some of which were not entirely agreeable; but there was one particular project of far-reaching importance with which she became involved. In 1891, together with A. H. Fried, a young Austrian who had become an enthusiastic supporter of the peace movement through reading *Lay down your Arms*, she founded on his initiative a monthly journal under the title *Die Waffen nieder!* (Lay down your Arms), the first number of which appeared on 1 February 1892 in Fried's small Berlin publishing house.

Alfred Hermann Fried was born in Vienna. As a schoolboy of sixteen he had seen in an art exhibition pictures of the Russian painter Vasili Vereshchagin which depicted battle scenes with great realism. Horrified at the wretchedness, suffering and terror which the artist had portrayed, Fried became a convinced opponent of all war. Since 1891 he had been working as a propagandist and journalist for the peace movement. In Berlin in 1892, where he was resident at the time, he founded the German Peace Society. Bertha Suttner, who had already been corresponding with Fried for some time, got to know him personally in that year, and her memoirs offer this picture of him :

> He received us when we arrived at the station, and this was the occasion on which I got to know the publisher and co-founder of my journal. A young man of twenty-eight years, filled with fire and enthusiasm, inspired with organisational zeal for the cause of peace. At once he worked out plans for making the best use of my stay in bringing about the planned formation of a society. A small private group was already in existence and this had to be turned into a proper peace association with the right to send representatives to this year's peace congress in Bern.[3]

But Bertha Suttner cannot have been completely happy with Fried's activities as a publisher, for after a little while the journal started appearing under the imprint of Pierson, her Dresden publisher. Her gifts as a journalist, which up until then had not been exploited to the full, found in *Die Waffen nieder!* a new rich area of activity. Since the journal was also the official organ of the bureau of the international parliamentary conferences, of the International Peace Bureau in Bern, and the Austrian Society, Bertha Suttner wrote reports for congresses and conferences, conducted a widespread correspondence with interested authors, took a stand on the events of the day, conducted campaigns against opponents of the society, published appeals, wrote critiques, news items and interviews, for example one with Count Muraviev, the Russian Foreign Minister, who played an important role in the preparations for the first peace conference at The Hague. The *Neue Freie Presse* published this interview on 25 October 1898 as its lead news item, and "partly on the same day, partly on the day following, the entire European press carried the story".[4] At the beginning she could call upon an extensive and prominent circle of contributors. But in its later years the journal lost its vigour and finally folded in 1899. This was partly attributable to the different paths the two organisations— the interparliamentary conferences and the international peace movement—took in the years 1891 to 1899, and partly also to the ever greater demands that the readership and also the membership of the ever-growing organisations imposed upon the contents of the journal.

It has already been mentioned that there was originally very close contact between the two organisations, not least because there was a substantial measure of joint membership. The conferences and congresses were held in the same location and virtually simultaneously. This was a matter of deliberate choice and was greatly welcomed by all concerned. Bertha Suttner wrote in the first issue of her journal in 1892 that

> it is to be hoped that for the future conference and congress might be held simultaneously, that is to say in alternate sessions, so that those participating in the deliberations of the one organisation might also be able to be present at the meetings of the other; for indeed most of the delegates who come together in the interparliamentary conference are also members of the peace societies of their respective countries; and so their voices should not fail to be heard in the discussions of the congress. For essentially the two bodies are no more than different manifestations of the same movement, and they have the closest possible mutual ties. The one grew from the other, and they are, so to speak, not unlike the upper and lower houses of the same parliament. . . . For the present the parliamentary and private committees must remain in the closest possible contact.[5]

But as early as 1897 the interparliamentary conference was taking place in Brussels between 7 and 12 August, whilst the peace congress held its sessions in Hamburg from 12 to 16 August, and the two organisations, which initially had been so intimately related by common ideals and personal contact, began to move further and further apart as the years went by. The following extract from a letter to Bertha Suttner in April 1898 demonstrates how a politician of the rank of Count Albert Apponyi regarded the situation : "My attitude to the peace movement is made unambiguously clear by my participation in the Interparliamentary Union; it is not possible for me to go beyond that. A certain division of activities is essential in the interest of the cause."[6] And the more practical importance the Interparliamentary Union assumed, the more the international peace society took on the characteristics of a private "club".

The group of interparliamentarians pressed for the realisation of two policies in the period before the First World War :

arbitration and disarmament. The former seemed to those parliamentarians well versed in practical politics more likely to be
achieved. In the 1891 conference in Rome there was already discussion on the prospect of establishing a permanent court of
arbitration, and at the 1895 Brussels conference Baron Descamps,
the organisation's president, drafted a plan in his "Mémoires aux
Puissances". These served as a basis for discussion in 1899 at the
peace conference at The Hague.

The Interparliamentary Union developed into an authoritative agency for international undertanding. It did not succeed in
preventing the First World War, but when, in 1915, the "Central
Organisation for a lasting Peace" was founded in Geneva, which
served as the focal point in preparation for the League of Nations
established in 1919, no less than forty interparliamentarians from
European countries took an active part. The Union continued
to serve in later years as a meeting place for parliamentarians
whose countries of origin were not members of the League of
Nations. And it also survived the Second World War. In Vienna
a conference took place in 1954, in the course of which the
representatives of the great powers were solemnly urged to take
all necessary measures for the restoration of Austrian independence. If at the present time the Union does not appear to figure
prominently in international affairs, there is still the future to
reveal whether new tasks lie before it, for example with regard
to the foundation of new parliaments in the developing countries.

Naturally the international peace movement was also fighting
for the realisation of its ideals: peace, an international federation, arbitration and disarmament. But it lacked an appropriate
arena, the practical opportunity for participating actively in
politics and having a direct influence on affairs. Its activities
became more and more restricted to the fields of journalism and
propaganda.

Bertha Suttner's experience as an editor was not great enough
in 1899 to measure up to the new situation which had been
brought about by the growing political significance of the Interparliamentary Union and the increased propaganda role of the
peace movement. She considered herself to be in a position where
she had to close down her journal and content herself with being
a collaborator on the *Friedens-Warte*, which Fried edited. Fried
underlined this change which had been wrought by circumstances in the words he wrote for the final edition: "No, *Die
Waffen nieder!* is not dying, it will live on. Its influence will

assume new forms, more modern, more appropriate to the age
and to present conditions, which correspond more nearly to the
more substantial demands of a movement which is now very
large." In the same issue, Bertha Suttner took her leave of her
readers with a promise to continue her journalistic work in the
future :

> Since the conference at The Hague, the movement has entered
> on a new stage; it now belongs to the world at large and to the
> world of politics. No longer is it just the province of isolated
> trail-blazers in need of an organ of news and information. These
> words are not in the nature of a farewell. I shall not put my
> pen down. Now as ever it will continue in the service of a
> common cause, which I hope to serve all the better by seeking
> to publish my observations and reports on the peace move-
> ment in the large circulation papers which are read by our
> opponents and the mass of the indifferent alike, than I have in
> the past by writing only for our convinced friends, the sub-
> scribers to this journal.[7]

Since Bertha Suttner could not be elected as a member of the
Austrian parliament, because at that time women still could not
stand for parliament, she naturally turned to political journalism.

She ventured into international journalism and made a success
of it. The list of names of the papers for which she wrote is
headed by the Viennese *Neue Freie Presse*, a liberal paper respected at home and abroad; then come the *Neues Wiener
Tagblatt*, the *Neues Wiener Journal, Die Zeit*, the *Öster-
reichische Rundschau*, the *Frankfurter Zeitung*, the *Berliner
Tagblatt*, the German language *New Yorker Staats-Zeitung*, the
Secolo, the *Courier Européen*, and many more. And naturally
Fried's journal, the *Friedens-Warte*, should be included in the list.
The extent of her journalistic activity is amazing. As the first
woman political journalist of exceptional quality, she played an
important role in international journalism. She had always taken
an interest in the press. She had recognised the importance of
this new world power at an early stage, and even during her
Caucasus days she underestimated neither the responsibility of
the journalist nor the possibilities of exercising influence upon the
reader. The hero of her book *Chess of Suffering*, the son of a
prince and an idealist seeking to improve the world and to relieve
the sufferings of mankind considers the thought of founding a
daily newspaper whose philosophy should be to "report the
events of the day with complete truthfulness and in such a light

as the philanthropist might wish to see for applying them for the benefit of a better tomorrow".[8] The aim of the paper would be to say "the truth, and nothing but the truth". It was to be a paper "which would hush nothing up in a cowardly manner, would leave nothing unsaid out of fear, would excuse nothing in order to curry favour, and would flatter no particular coterie or class".[9] He continues triumphantly: "My newspaper—it will give me a powerful means for the propagation of those ideas which I confidently expect will overcome some of the principal causes of human suffering."[10] Bertha Suttner's enthusiastic newspaper founder continues: "The new spirit demands its public organs . . . In the function of editor there must be something of the dignity of the High Priest who is sensible of the weighty responsibility bestowed upon one with such great power."[11]

Her most violent attacks were reserved for the corrupt press, the press that can be bought, the press which was heightening the danger of war and stirring men up with false information. "A yellow pestilence—worse than the threatened yellow peril of the invading Mongol hordes, worse than the yellow fever—is devastating the spirit of the community: namely, the agitating, slandering, power-adulating yellow press."[12]

She had always taken her journalistic activities very seriously, working through the night when she had to meet a deadline and holding fast to her principles, even when, as in her later years, writing no longer came easily to her.

NOTES

1. *Die Waffen nieder!* 1893, no. 2.
2. A. H. Fried, *Die moderne Friedensbewegung*, Leipzig, 1907, p. 73.
3. *Memoiren*, p. 241
4. *Die Waffen nieder!* 1898, no. 12.
5. *Ibid.*, 1892, no. 1.
6. Collection Suttner-Fried (Da 1–25).
7. *Die Waffen nieder!* 1899, no. 12.
8. *Schach der Qual*, Dresden, 1906, p. 93. (The rather odd title of this novel—which she subtitles "ein Phantasiestück", a fantastical tale—derives from the vision of its protagonist, Prince Roland, for whom the formula "Schach der Qual" epitomises the struggle between the forces of good and ill, happiness and suffering, as represented by the black and white opposing forces on the chessboard.—Translator.)
9. *Ibid.*, p. 85.
10. *Ibid.*, p. 90.
11. *Ibid.*, p. 93.
12. "Was ich dämmern sehe", in *Stimmen und Gestalten*, Leipzig, 1907, p. 79.

PEACE CONFERENCE IN THE HAGUE 1899

Shortly before the close of the last century, an event took place which the friends of peace greeted with jubilation, triumph even. In May 1899 the first peace conference was convened at The Hague. It was regarded as an event as epoch-making as the Congress of Vienna, held almost a hundred years before. Bertha Suttner and all friends of peace saw in this first peace and disarmament conference a significant milestone in the development of the peace movement, which they now considered as having entered "the sphere of practical politics" because this conference had been constituted at the highest diplomatic level. Still, she added cautiously, "this does not mean that the raison d'être of our movement has vanished".[1] A group of unofficial organisations had thus succeeded in playing an important role in international politics.

When, on 28 August 1898 the St. Petersburg government gazette published the official announcement which has gone into the history books as the "Czar's Manifesto", Bertha Suttner was among those to greet it with great enthusiasm as a splendid victory for the endeavours of the peace movement.

Russia's Foreign Minister, Count Muraviev, had issued a circular which contained the following important proposals:

> The maintenance of a general peace and a possible reduction of excessive armaments, a burden which weighs heavily on all nations, are in the present world situation an ideal towards which the endeavours of all governments must be directed. . . . In the conviction that this noble objective is in accordance with the fundamental interests and just desires of all powers, the imperial government takes the view that the present moment is extremely propitious for seeking through international discussion the most effective means of securing the benefits of a true and lasting peace for all the nations and above all to set up an upper limit to the continuing growth in armaments. . . . Dominated by this feeling, his majesty has been pleased to command me to propose to all governments whose representatives are accredited at the imperial court that a conference be called together with the purpose of discussing these weighty issues. . . . It would unite the endeavours of all the

nations in a powerful alliance honestly concerned to bring about the victory of the grand design of world peace over all forms of strife and discord.[2]

As soon as this manifesto was made public, Bertha Suttner threw herself behind the cause and embarked on a systematic propaganda campaign : "Now comes the arduous task of doing one's utmost to ensure that the success of this conference, for the institution of which we have prayed and voted so long, should also be assured",[3] she writes in her memoirs, and continues :

> Through meetings and public statements, our Austrian Society has ensured that our wholehearted support for this initiative has been made unambiguously clear, and for several weeks the headline "International Peace Crusade" has appeared regularly in the *Neue Freie Presse* and the *Neues Wiener Tagblatt.*[3]

The other friends of peace also launched intensive propaganda campaigns with great enthusiasm. The general meeting of the Bern International Peace Bureau which was in session in Turin at the time of the publication of the Czar's manifesto resolved upon an intensive publicity campaign in the spirit of the manifesto. In England a good two hundred public meetings were held, at which statesmen, parliamentarians and representatives of the church spoke on the objectives of the planned conference. The pacifist William T. Stead founded a weekly journal in England called *War against War*, in which no less a figure than Pope Leo XIII, through his spokesman Cardinal Rampolla, let his wish be known that all the nations should be united in a brotherly bond. In Munich and Berlin, committees for organising meetings on the peace conference were set up, and in France, Italy and Scandinavia great excitement was generated by the prospect of the conference. "These public manifestations of the will of the nations for peace constitute a magnificent prelude to the conference", was the way one diplomat expressed it in the most approving terms.

The events leading up to this manifesto can be traced back to the year 1896, when Russian representatives took part in the peace congress, which was a particularly lavish affair, and in the sessions of the interparliamentary conference in Budapest. Consul Basily was among their number, and he reported back to his government as a convinced friend of peace "and gave a sympathetic report".[5] And in addition, the following resolution was passed in a session on 22 September :

The seventh interparliamentary conference calls upon all civilised states to summon a diplomatic conference to discuss the question of international arbitration, in which the work of the Interparliamentary Union should serve as a basis for further resolutions.[6]

The most fundamental and crucial impetus for Czar Nicholas, however, must have come, as the Austrian Ambassador from St. Petersburg reported, in the book by His Excellency the Imperial Russian Councillor of State and millionaire J. v. Bloch *The War of the Future: its technological, political and economic Significance*, a six-volume work totalling some four thousand pages. "He examines the ideas of Bertha von Suttner from a purely military and scientific viewpoint and brilliantly expounds the folly of a European war and the necessity for a certain degree of disarmament", a "private letter" from St. Petersburg of 31 August 1898 to the Foreign Ministry in Vienna reports. "His first audience with the Czar lasted two hours", the letter continues, "and his Imperial Majesty has commanded the publication of the text, and the work has been in the bookshops for two weeks. As a result, Herr von Bloch has been received by the Czar on five further occasions in long audiences, and later in May on many occasions by the Czarina."[7]

The Austrian court and state archives in Vienna reveal that the diplomats of all countries to which the invitation was sent out were unanimous about the Czar's sincerity, but not about the motives which had led the Russian ministers to send out the manifesto of their imperial master at this particular point in time and to work towards this conference whose objective was disarmament or an arms standstill. In individual embassies there was much puzzlement; and their views were reported back to Vienna by the Austrian Ambassadors and other diplomatic representatives. These reports offer a picture of the different lines of conjecture the diplomats were pursuing, each according to his own nationality and temperament.

Thus the British Ambassador in St. Petersburg Sir Charles Scott was recorded as taking the view that

he did not doubt the honesty of the young Czar's initiative which was taken under the influence of a certain Bloch and of the Budapest peace conference under the chairmanship of General Türr; but his advisers had clearly been pursuing other objectives than the noble aims which his Imperial Majesty had in view. The bad harvest and the plight of the population were even more serious than had been realised. Witte had promised the 160 millions for artillery purposes, and did not now want to break his word. Russia was therefore dependent on a large influx of foreign capital, and France would not increase the seven millions already paid to Russia. So an approach was made to London which gave the firm reply that Britain would not divert a penny piece towards Russia until such time as the Czar's régime gave proof positive of its peaceful intentions; British capital should not be used for strategic railway links, harbour fortifications and other armaments which could be turned against England, but only for agricultural and industrial purposes. It was the purpose of the Muraviev circular to provide such proof. That is the sceptical view of the British Ambassador.[8]

The following report was sent to Vienna from Berlin :

... and for this reason we are disposed to search out the more opportunist views of Witte's policy which would certainly need a lengthy period of peace and new sources of credit for Russia in order to guarantee economic supremacy in east Asia and the construction of a huge railway network with both a large war and peacetime potential.[9]

And from Rumania :

Mr. Sturdza is inclined to attribute not just humanitarian motives to the famous circular but also to see in it a carefully considered policy based on self-interest.[10]

In London, the Austrian Ambassador spoke to Under-Secretary Bertie about Russian foreign policy and reported back to Vienna:

Bertie, who indicated that his conversation with me was off the record, had some quite sharp things to say about the Russian government. Czar Nicholas was in his view entirely in the hands of his ministers who, paying lip-service to the Czar's humanitarian ideals, were in reality pursuing just one goal, namely, to persuade the other powers, especially Britain, to curb their armaments programme until Russia had completed the construction of the Siberian railway and had succeeded in raising more loans. The difficulties which Russia had come up against in her attempts to raise money were the real reason behind the disarmament proposals.[11]

In January 1899 the eight-point programme of the planned conference was made public by the Russian Foreign Minister : six of the points concerned war, and only two of its provisions related to reductions in armaments and peaceful resolution of international disputes.

After the immediate sceptical reaction had passed and The Hague was finally settled on as the location for the conference, opinions were being voiced to the effect that the wisest counsel would be to bow to the inevitable. So in Paris for example,

> the view gradually gained acceptance that it was not politic to accept the disgrace of being implicated in the possible failure of the conference by excessive emphasis on reservations with reference to their undying right to the two lost provinces (Alsace–Lorraine). . . . They felt they ought to get used to the idea of the conference, because it was after all no more than an "international talking-shop" which would have no immediate practical outcome.[12]

The German Ambassador in Paris, Count Münster, was also sceptical about the successful outcome of the coming conference. The Austrian Ambassador wrote :

> He and I both take the view that it is strongly in the interest of the big powers to prevent The Hague conference from ending in a fiasco. A fiasco would create an international scandal, and this would do nothing but harm to the status of the powers.[13]

Count Zichy, Austrian Ambassador to Munich, was of the opinion that "the participation of the powers in The Hague conference is no more and no less than an act of courtesy towards the Czar".[14] On 28 April 1899 a discussion took place in the Foreign Ministry in Vienna, shortly before the departure of the Austrian delegation for The Hague, which it was reported stressed the "difficult and delicate" nature of the situation, for in the present state of affairs there appeared to be no prospect of any far-reaching results. "On the other hand," observed the Austrian Minister of the Exterior Goluchovski,

> if the conference handles the question of arbitration skilfully it will then find itself able to give the public at large the impression that the work of the conference has despite everything arrived at a positive result.[15]

The scepticism of the diplomats was in sharp contrast to the great enthusiasm and sense of victory of the friends of peace who, like Bertha Suttner, were making for The Hague, "the place where peace is to be born ! That is indeed the finest goal which fate could have offered me after my hopes and longings over the years."[16] She was anxious during the conference to stay in the immediate vicinity of the conference chamber where the questions are discussed which have for many years been the object of our study and our propaganda work, and which constitute our most precious ideals.[17]

Two further representatives of Austrian pacifism present were Baron P. Pirquet and A. H. Fried. Some pacifists played a very important role in The Hague, among them J. von Bloch, the author of the book on modern warfare, and William T. Stead, the strict Quaker and tireless campaigner for the cause of world peace, who died so tragically aboard the Titanic.

The pacifists were unable to participate in the conference itself, because its proceedings were held behind closed doors, but they wanted at least to try to enter into personal contact with the delegates and perhaps exercise some influence upon the decisions taken.

On 18 May 1899 the formal opening session took place, at which the Dutch Foreign Minister greeted the representatives of the twenty-six governments. In one of the places allocated to the fifteen journalists who were admitted sat Bertha Suttner, the only woman in the room. She wrote an account of the conference in The Hague in book form, under the title *The Hague Peace Conference*, which records the shifting pattern of opinions, the work of the individual commissions and the social life of the conference as well as reporting on the "lobbying" outside the conference hall proper. Bertha Suttner was present at all the receptions and she knew the most important and influential personalities present.

> Baroness von Suttner's salon in The Hague was the focal point for all those interested in what was going on, for delegates, journalists and interviewers, who managed to find out a great deal of things and make them public despite the fact that the proceedings were officially secret.[18]

For the friends of peace and the journalists she was "the Baroness von Suttner", the authoress of the book *Lay down your Arms*, a fellow-campaigner and colleague. She was interviewed and received many letters and requests for assistance. She records in her memoirs that she found it difficult to keep abreast of her correspondence.

> Here in The Hague I have received as many letters, telegrams and other material to read as normally come my way in a full year. Advice, proposals, guaranteed methods for

securing peace. And I am supposed to digest all that and put it across to the conference delegates. Even the inventors of airships and flying machines send me their plans.[19]

The correspondents of the *Frankfurter Zeitung*, the *Echo de Paris* and of *Le Figaro* were among those who interviewed her, and when Dr. Frischauer, the editor of the *Neue Freie Presse*, left The Hague, he gave her the task of reporting on anything of interest in the "telegrams and correspondence" section of the paper.[20] She had evidently sought to obtain a regular reporting job from other papers, and this casts an interesting light on her position half-way between press and society, especially because the diplomats conducted themselves in a most unfriendly manner towards the press during the peace conference. A letter dated 31 May 1899 to Bertha Suttner from Arthur Levysohn, the editor in chief of the *Berliner Tageblatt*, expresses the position in no uncertain terms:

> ... that in the view of the hostile attitude which the members of the conference have thought fit to adopt towards the press, I do not consider it right that the journalists should allow themselves to be disgraced by having to resort to lobbying the various statesmen.[21]

For the diplomats, who at that time were almost to a man members of the nobility of their country of origin, she was Baroness Suttner, née Countess Kinsky, who at the same time happened to be a writer who wrote for newspapers. She was held to be the most important representative of Austrian pacifism who, as lady president of the Austrian Peace Society, had contacts with all other pacifists as well as with many politicians. She was a well-known figure, and there is no doubt that she was caught up in the game of diplomatic intrigue.

In this context she writes in her memoirs:

> Afternoon reception with Monsieur and Madame d'Estournelles. The conference continues on its course. D. Andrew White is deep in conversation with Count Münster. Then he comes across to me and says: "If, Baroness, you have any connections with people of influence, now is the time to make use of them. No stone must be left unturned if we are to overcome the difficulties that lie before us. Our conference has come to a crucial point on the most important issue before us, namely the question of the court of arbitration, and that is what I have just been discussing with Count Münster." All I could promise him was

that I would ask one of my friends in The Hague, who is highly regarded by the Grand Duke of Baden, the uncle of the German Kaiser, to approach the prince about this knife-edge situation.[22]

The deliberations on the court of arbitration had made a deep impact on all concerned. The Austrian delegate, Professor Dr. Lammasch, an expert on international law, reported that when Sir Julian Pauncefote read out his proposal that a permanent court of arbitration be set up, all those present felt the "breath of history"[23] upon them. But because of objections raised by the German delegate Professor Zorn in the arbitration court commission, the negotiations had reached an impasse and had to be interrupted for a fortnight. The German delegation seems to have taken part in the conference with a severely limited brief and with considerable reservations on the part of their government, and they made no efforts to conceal this. It is true that Professor Stengel had been attached to the delegation; he was "a thoroughly competent teacher who had written some solid handbooks on Prussian, Bavarian and German administrative law",[24] and had been sent to The Hague, but he was not very tactful or diplomatic—shortly before the conference began he had published a pamphlet on the subject of an enduring peace, in which he came out strongly against the idea of disarmament. And Bertha Suttner records that, at a soirée held by the chief lady-in-waiting of the Queen of the Netherlands, the German delegation was the only one which did not do her the honour of approaching her.

> Count Münster treats me as if I wasn't there. When Professor Stengel talks about the "comic personalities" of the peace movement in his pamphlet, against whose grotesque ideas and conduct he warns his readers in the strongest terms, he evidently includes me among them.[25]

All these observations give a clear enough indication of the real "game behind the scenes", the significance of the delegates' consultations in the corridors, and the mutual relationships between delegates and pacifists. Politics went on behind closed doors, meetings were arranged, and people were hopeful of a positive outcome, even though many shared the scornful view of Kaiser Wilhelm that The Hague was a most appropriate meeting place for a conference dedicated to such utopian and mystical objectives, since it was the residence of a youthful virgin Queen.

At that time the Kaiser could not possibly have foreseen that this same Queen, out of the selfsame high principles that had led her to hold this congress within the walls of her residence, would later grant him asylum under tragic circumstances.

As the diplomats had predicted, the sole important outcome of the conference was the establishment of a permanent court of arbitration, which was to be accessible at all times, and which was to exercise its function in accordance with the rules laid down in the convention, if the parties to a dispute did not have any mutual arrangements of their own for this purpose. It was resolved to set up an International Bureau in The Hague with lists of arbitration judges, but the idea of a court in permanent session was not realised. The "Hague Tribunal", which at first was housed in modest accommodation, only later received its own spacious palace of justice in 1913, through the generosity of the American philanthropist Carnegie. The permanent court of arbitration was to do important work in the years after the First World War and resolved several disputes under international law. Since the end of the Second World War its significance has waned; but it is possible that it may gain in importance once more since there are moves afoot to give the permanent court power to deal with disputes between states and private undertakings.

The weeks spent in The Hague must be counted among the happiest periods of Bertha Suttner's life. In her eyes, the conference itself was a victory and a triumph for the ideals of the peace movement. The respect with which all received her and the unquestioning terms of equality on which she was treated confirmed her in the view that both her work for the peace movement as well as her personality as a writer and journalist were being given due recognition. She must also have derived considerable satisfaction from her social successes. Since, despite occasional assertions to the contrary, she was not greatly enamoured of the quiet home life, but ventured out into the world at large where she was happiest amidst the bustle of congresses and conferences, The Hague conference was an experience after her own heart, as her accounts clearly indicate. And also, in her capacity as lady president of the Peace Society of Vienna, the capital city of the Austro-Hungarian monarchy, she assumed a position of international importance. It was no longer possible to disregard her. Her opinions on world events, whether published in articles or expressed in speeches, carried considerable weight, since she was regarded as the Austrian spokeswoman for pacifism, and as a pacifist she was now taken seriously and respected.

NOTES

1. *Memoiren*, p. 100.
2. *Die Haager Friedenskonferenz*, Dresden, 1901, p. iv.
3. *Memoiren*, p. 400.
4. *Die Haager Friedenskonferenz*, p. 10.
5. *Memoiren*, p. 362.
6. *Ibid.*, p. 360.
7. Haus-, Hof- und Staatsarchiv, Pol. Archiv X/143, Liasse VI/A, private letter from Petersburg, 31 August 1898.
8. Pol. Archiv X/143, Liasse VI/A, report no. 96B from Petersburg, dated 3 October–21 November 1898.
9. Report no. 34 from Berlin, 2 September 1898.
10. Report no. 38c from Sinaia, 10 September 1898.
11. Pol. Archiv X/144, Liasse VI/B, report no 2D from London, 19 January 1899.
12. Pol. Archiv X/143, Liasse VI/A, Report no. 54A–B from Paris, 21 September 1898.
13. Pol. Archiv X/144, Liasse VI/B, private letter by Wenkheim from Paris, 1 April 1899.
14. Report no. 11 from Munich, 7 April 1899.
15. Protocol of the discussion in the Hague conference held on 28 April 1899 in the Ministry of External Affairs.
16. *Die Haager Friedenskonferenz*, p. 1.
17. *Ibid.*, p. 1ff.
18. Christian Menier, *Die Haager Friedenskonferenz*, Munich, 1905, p. 25.
19. *Memoiren*, p. 465.
20. *Die Haager Friedenskonferenz*, p. 91.
21. Library of the United Nations Geneva, Peace Archives, Collection Suttner-Fried (Fa 5).
22. *Memoiren*, p. 469.
23. M. Lammasch and H. Sperl (eds.), *Heinrich Lammasch. Seine Aufzeichnungen, sein Wirken und seine Politik*, Leipzig, 1922, p. 17.
24. Pol. Archiv X/144, Liasse VI/B, report no. 11 from Munich, 7 April 1899.
25. *Memoiren*, p. 453.

THE TESTAMENT OF ALFRED NOBEL

The period which began with the foundation of the Austrian Society of the Friends of Peace in 1891 and ended with the death of her husband in 1902, a decade of the most intensive work and steadily growing publicity in which Bertha and Arthur Suttner came to number among the world's most prominent pacifists, could have been the happiest time of her life. But fate willed otherwise.

After years of exile the Suttners had been only too anxious to take up residence in Harmannsdorf, the family seat, and after a long banishment they were delighted to return to the bosom of their large family. At first Bertha Suttner must have found that belonging to this family circle had its attractions. But the more she became a well-known personality of the literary and later of the political world, the less easy she found it to remain on good terms with her husband's relatives for all the mutual affection that may have existed.

Bertha Suttner's diaries are almost complete from 1897, and offer a comprehensive picture of her daily activities, her work and her feelings, and in their pages she can be found complaining about the restricting atmosphere in Harmannsdorf: "The days speed past without interest."[1]—"Life here really is boring. I am no stranger to boredom, but family life here is tedious in the extreme."[2]—"Living at home is so drab."[3]—"We ought to be more in Vienna to keep our contacts alive and establish new ones. Out here we are not part of the world any more."[4] Financial worries too were on the increase. The Suttners' income from their literary and journalistic activities was not meagre, but Bertha Suttner records that the two of them had to work on as hard as ever they could. "There we sat of an evening sharing the same working table, usually until midnight and after, and wrote on and on." But their earnings were nowhere near enough to ward off bankruptcy; they could only postpone the evil day, "for the Harmannsdorf stone business went from bad to worse, and this was a source of great despondency for the whole family as the fearful prospect of having to leave their beloved family home came ever closer. One sacrifice after another was made—

and our substantial literary income was swallowed up along with the rest."[5]

Every page of the diaries at this time contains complaints about the financial difficulties her husband had to confront; since the father's death in 1898 he had controlled the family business singlehanded, and had to contend with quarrels among members of the family. Every day brought its mention of the burden of worry, the fear of bankruptcy, the prospect of selling the family residence, much loved as a home despite all the anxieties, a prospect they always seemed to manage to postpone by means of the income their writing brought them. In February 1897 she noted: "Slept badly because of three things on my mind: my work, the worries of the family and the house, and also anxiety about the state of things in Europe."[6]

So it was more than understandable that after the death of Alfred Nobel in 1896, with whom she had been in lively correspondence since their Paris meeting in 1875, Bertha Suttner took a considerable interest in the settlement of his will and the establishment of the Nobel foundation as well as in the presentation of the first prizes, and she was bitterly disappointed to find that she had been passed over. It was a matter of life and death for the Suttner family: for if in 1901 Bertha Suttner had been accorded the prize when her husband was still alive, the property would have remained in the hands of the family. In March 1897 she wrote:

> Not doing a scrap of work. Have seen parents again, a disagreeable affair because there was no cause for cheerfulness. If only I had received the Nobel inheritance, then what could I have done! But nothing plus nothing take away nothing leaves nothing.[7]

Or again: "One day I'll make it, I think. I'm laying my plans now. It will have to be shared. But it will be enough to keep me in my old age. That is not so bad."[8]

According to how people took this woman who for her time was so modern, so emancipated and so eccentric, her friendly relationship with Nobel was either seen as exaggerated in its importance, or surrounded with cloying sentimentality, as was the case in the film *Das Herz der Welt* which was made after the Second World War, or even trivialised as in the biography of Nobel written by H. Schück and R. Sohlmann.[9] In it Nobel is depicted as a gifted inventor and skilled businessman, but also as an extravagant idealist, a poet who took Shelley as his model, who regarded him as a kindred spirit in his overwhelming idealism, his pacifism and his all-embracing love for his fellow men. Manuscripts of Nobel's creative writings have survived, among them a youthful poem in the style of Shelley, novels and fragments of novels, dramas and sketches of dramas, which take as their theme Nobel's political, religious and literary opinions. Nobel's will is seen simply as a natural consequence of his philosophy of life. The authors of the biography deny any direct influence on Nobel from Bertha Suttner.

A study of the available material, either in published form, like Bertha Suttner's memoirs, or the as yet unpublished documents preserved in archives—for example, her correspondence with Nobel—makes it possible to establish the considerable extent to which Bertha Suttner's convictions influenced Nobel's will and the momentous section of that document which led to the institution of the Nobel Peace Prize. Bertha Suttner's statements in her memoirs are essentially reliable because she bases them on her diary entries. Perhaps she twists some things to her advantage and places many of her actions in an excessively favourable light, but relatively minor shifts of emphasis such as these do not prejudice the fundamental honesty of what she records. And according to her memoirs three personal meetings with Nobel were of especial significance.

The first was in 1875 when she met Nobel in Paris, and conversed with him in the course of her employment as his secretary and housekeeper. She had a mere week in which to come to know him, and she always recalled with pleasure the interesting discussions she was able to hold with him. A score of years later she reminded Nobel in a letter of that "remarkable little tale" and sketched a life-like portrait of the character of this man who had almost become a legend in his own lifetime :

> Often we turn our eyes back into the past, and let old memories pass before our gaze. That is what happened to me this morning when I was musing for a while—I thought back to the autumn of 1875, exactly twenty years ago now. . . . That was when I met him. What a strange little tale—for it was not long enough to be a novel—or rather sketch for a psychological study : a thinker, a poet, a human being, bitter and good, gay and sad, whose thoughts ranged far but who had his moments of foreboding, a man who passionately loved the great sweep of the human imagination and despised the pettiness of human

folly, a man who understood everything and hoped for nothing :
that is how you appeared to me then. And the passage of
twenty years has not clouded the memory. . . . I called it all back
to mind and remained sunk in thought—and while I was thinking it occurred to me to put my thoughts on paper—and that is
all for now, B. Suttner, 29 October 1895.[10]

Soon after her return to Europe Nobel himself almost visited
Harmannsdorf. In a letter he states that he had made a short
stay in Vienna, but had unfortunately not met Bertha Suttner in
that city, and did not venture to travel out to Harmannsdorf :

Here I am in Vienna, but you are not here, and they tell me
that you are not a frequent visitor in this city. But I fear to
cause any trouble to you if I were to come to Harmannsdorf,
and in matters like this I am as shy as the most sensitive
woman.[11]

During their stay in Paris between 1886 and 1887, the
Suttners once more entered into personal contact with Nobel;
and they visited him in his residence in the Avenue Malakoff.
Arthur Suttner was interested in the scientific work of the
Swedish inventor, and Bertha Suttner discussed his literary activi-
ties with him.

The last and most important meeting took place in Zurich in
1892. In August of that year the world peace congress and the
fourth interparliamentary conference were being held in Bern,
and Bertha Suttner had hoped to see Nobel participating in these
gatherings. But he had declined her pressing invitation, largely
because his attitude towards the successful outcome of these
various conferences was sceptical in the extreme.

"My factories," he once said to Bertha Suttner, "may well
bring a more rapid end to war than your congresses; on the day
when two army divisions find themselves capable of wiping each
other out in a single second all civilised nations will draw back
from the brink and disband their forces."[12] But he did invite
Baron and Baroness Suttner to be his guests in Zurich. During
this brief stay there took place the boat trip on the Lake of
Zurich which was of "historical" importance for the Nobel foundation, and in the course of which, according to Bertha Suttner,
Nobel made an observation on the manner in which a large
fortune should be distributed on the death of its owner which
pointed to the way in which his own will was to be formulated
some years later : "It is not proper for the rich," she records

Nobel as having said, "to leave their fortune to their relations."
And he added : "Inherited fortunes I consider to be 'misfortunes', because their effect is inhibiting. A large amassed fortune
should revert to the community for the use of society at large."[13]
Bertha Suttner records Nobel's views on the efforts of the peace
movement in these terms :

> Of course I don't have any reservations about the cause itself
> or its worthiness; what I do doubt is whether it will meet with
> any real success. Nor am I clear as to how their societies and
> congresses will ever achieve their ends. Instruct me and con-
> vince me in this matter—and then I will do great things for the
> movement.[14]

Even before Nobel had made that declaration in Zurich,
Bertha Suttner had written enthusiastic letters to him about her
successes as lady president of the Austrian Peace Society, and
Nobel had replied in the most courteous terms, offering her his
congratulations and made her a donation of 2,000 francs so that
she could undertake the journey to Rome in 1891. So those
words spoken on the Lake of Zurich must have been an even
greater incentive for her to keep Nobel very closely informed
about her work and the progress of the peace movement, with
the object of overcoming all his doubts about its practical
effectiveness.

As far as is known, the correspondence consists of sixteen
letters from Nobel between 1881–96, and a much larger number
from Bertha Suttner spanning the years 1891–96.[15] It is possible
that this numerical imbalance can be attributed to the fact that
she destroyed some of Nobel's letters because of their content,
but it is much more probable that she simply misplaced them in
the untidy clutter of her documents : "This afternoon I was rum-
maging about among my papers and made a valuable find—the
letter which Nobel wrote to me in 1891 about *Lay down your
Arms*."[16] Or perhaps she just threw the letters away : in her
diaries she notes that she rescued Nobel's very last letter from her
waste paper basket. "Looked in the waste paper basket for
Nobel's last, doubly precious letter and have found it. That is a
real joy for me."[17]

The style of her letters is a delight, her attempts to win him
over conducted with great vitality, her reports on the successes
of the peace movement composed enthusiastically and with
psychological adroitness, her pleas for financial assistance for

the Bern Bureau or her Vienna society sometimes expressed
obliquely, but often quite bluntly.

> Here are some printed documents. I am sending you these
> from time to time so as to keep you informed about the move-
> ment. If only you would become enthusiastic about our work!
> Your generous gift has been of great benefit to our society,
> and the committee thanks you sincerely. A few of the news-
> papers could not restrain themselves from comment on the ex-
> ceptional selflessness of an inventor of war machines who allies
> himself with a peace society.[18]

That was what she wrote shortly after the stay in Zurich. She
was depressed at his lack of understanding and sought to defend
herself: "Do not keep calling our peace plan a dream. Progress
on the path to justice is certainly no dream, it is a law of civilisation."[19] Her search for his support and attention is not without
a strain of coquetry:

> No, my letters should not be pressed to the heart as the precious
> manuscripts of their charming author; their purpose is simply
> to arouse an echo of sympathy, not for the author, but for the
> work that is so dear to her heart. You can throw all these pieces
> of paper into the waste paper basket but do preserve in your
> heart of hearts her voice that says to you: here is a woman
> who despite the indifference and opposition her ideas met with
> has persisted in her task, a woman who has confidence in me.[20]

And in what was probably the last letter he received before he
died she requests—demands even—a million francs for the
movement.

> Dear friend,
>   Your letter saddened me. You give me sad news, and then you
> tell me that you love no one who holds the first place in my
> respect and inclination. A sick heart? I pity you, for that is a
> disease which causes great pain and poses a constant danger.
> Only a man who knows the ways of the world as you do could
> speak so off-handedly about such a matter.
>   But no heart? That is untrue. Perhaps not for me—but
> even here I have proof to the contrary; well, I do concede that
> your heart is immovable towards certain people. But you are
> neither hard nor wicked, for that would deserve the title "heart-
> less", and in my experience this is only true of people who have
> no head either.
>   You say that the progress of the peace movement is attri-
> butable to the "warmongers." Perhaps in some respects and

a warning to generations to come. But what has been achieved so far is the direct result of individual initiatives : what Hodgson Pratt, Randall Cremer, Ducommun, Passy and perhaps Frau Suttner as well have done has been to prepare the way for those institutions through which we now have an Interparliamentary Union, a peace movement and the ratification of a permanent arbitration court agreement between Britain and the United States. It has always been individuals who have brought about great achievements of this order : Dunant founded the Red Cross, Stephan established the Postal Union; and today one of us is able to set in train a peace conference on an inter-governmental level and the institution of an international tribunal. It would suffice if two or three countries set an example.

Well, I have played my part in all this; at my suggestion the Rome congress let a certain line of discussion drop which could have brought the whole fragile edifice crashing about our ears, and I was behind the original idea for the establishment of the Bern Bureau, which would otherwise have not come about; I was responsible for the movement gaining a foothold in Austria and Germany, and for the foundation of the society in Budapest. . . . If I look more closely at my endeavours, I must confess that I should have been able to do nothing, absolutely nothing, without the assistance which you have rendered and which you continue to give our work. We cannot do without the power of money, which has the same kind of effect as melinite.[21] Give Archimedes a lever or give our Bureau a million—and we will lift the world off its hinges. At this moment I have a certain measure of prestige in literary and political circles—if I also had the means to travel to Russia or Berlin or Paris, if we could publish pamphlets and newspaper articles by the hundred thousand, then it is my firm conviction that the twentieth century would see the setting up of a lasting institution of peace. That is why I beg for one thing on my bended knees : never withdraw your support from us, not even beyond the grave which awaits us all. I have recently lost a dear friend, one of the pillars of our Vienna society, Count Rudolf Hoyos, a poet, a noble spirit—I was grief-stricken. God grant that you are not taken from us. This letter needs no answer. I shall continue to keep you up to date with printed material. B.S.[22]

Nobel always replied in a charming if somewhat reserved manner, blaming pressure of work and ill-health for the infrequency of his replies. But the tone of his letters is always heartfelt and personal, and her appeals clearly did not fall on deaf ears.

On 7 January 1893, probably recollecting their conversation on the Lake of Zurich, he wrote :

My dear friend,
A good year for you and the noble campaign you are conducting with such resolution against ignorance and folly. In my will I shall set aside a portion of my estate for a prize to be awarded once every five years (up to a total of six, for if there has been no success in reforming the status quo within the space of thirty years, then we shall inevitably revert to barbarity). The prize is to be awarded to the individual who has advanced furthest in the direction of a peaceful Europe. I am not saying along the path to disarmament, for this will only be achieved gradually and after lengthy deliberations. What is possible and should be within our reach, is that all states should undertake together to attack aggression by any individual state. This would render war impossible and compel even the most brutal and irrational power to seek refuge in peaceful negotiation. If the Triple Alliance embraced all states instead of just three, then peace would be assured for centuries.[23]

It was in November 1895 that Nobel drew up his will which contained the momentous decision to fund a prize for the man or woman who had done most to bring the nations together, to disband or reduce standing armies, and to institute and further the work of peace congresses.

The extracts that have been quoted from his letters indicate beyond all doubt on the one hand, that he was much concerned about bringing peace to the world, that he himself sought to achieve peace among the nations through his own inventions on the basis of their deterrent value, and on the other hand, that he fully supported the endeavours of the peace movement, of whose activities Bertha Suttner kept him so fully informed. Despite his sceptical attitude towards the activities of the idealists, despite his disapproval of their plans for the establishment of a binding court of arbitration, despite too his doubts about the possibility of putting an effective disarmament policy into practice, he gave full recognition to the achievements of Bertha Suttner and those who shared her convictions.

His resolve not to restrict the beneficiaries of his estate to representatives of the world of science, but also to set up prizes for those who, in his own words, worked towards "the disbanding of armies and the formation and proliferation of peace congresses", can in the first instance be traced back to the efforts and influence of Bertha Suttner.

This was also the sincere opinion of Nobel's friends and the supporters of the peace movement. In the journal *Die Waffen nieder!* an article from *Temps* was published called "Autour du Testament", which contained the following:

> Nobel was firmly convinced that work and knowledge were the well-springs of human happiness. He believed that scientific progress would inject a new spirit into human society, act as a civilising force and make war a thing of the past. He had a horror of cannon, of militarism, of all the paraphernalia of war. Frau von Suttner had played her part in inspiring such sentiments in him, her book *Lay down your Arms* made a considerable impression. . . . and thus the inventor of dynamite became an advocate of the peace movement. On the one hand, he was working to produce instruments of mass murder, on the other he condemned the use of artillery. He devoted the vast sums of money paid to him by the Ministers of War to the pacifist activities of Frau von Suttner.[24]

Some of Nobel's heirs fought a bitter battle against his will. If it had not been for the uncompromising stand taken by members of the family resident in Russia, it would scarcely have been possible to have Nobel's instructions ratified and the Nobel foundation set up, or at least, not in the form which it took. Emanuel Nobel, a nephew of the dead man, renounced millions in order that Alfred Nobel's wish should be respected, although he was urged by the King of Sweden himself to protest against the will, "because it damages the cause of peace" as the Storting might employ the money for anti-Swedish purposes (a fear caused by the current tension between Norway and Sweden which at that time still formed a single state).[25] Emanuel Nobel had visited Bertha Suttner on 26 October 1900 in Harmannsdorf and told her these details about the fight for the confirmation of his uncle's will.

Bertha Suttner became involved in the discussion surrounding the interpretation of the will. The problem was whether the peace prize should be given to organisations or individuals. She campaigned for the prize to be given every time to individual pacifists of merit, believing she was expressing Nobel's wishes, but she did not have her way. In the years that followed, it was possible to present the prize singly or divide it among individuals or institutions.

It was quite understandable that Bertha Suttner hoped to be the recipient of one of the first Nobel Prizes. But she generously recognised that the first two to win the prize, Passy, and Dunant, the founder of the Red Cross, had as big a claim to the reward as herself, although she had some reservations in respect of Dunant, because he was not a campaigner for peace in the strict sense of the term. It was not until 1905 that she herself received the prize—after the many intrigues directed against her had been overcome—as a result of the moral and practical support of her friends from many countries who campaigned tirelessly for her to be accorded the prize. It was awarded to her alone, and she received it on 18 April 1906 in Christiana (Oslo). The news of the Storting's decision came to her in Wiesbaden, where she was making a stop in the course of her great lecture tour through Germany.

> Wiesbaden, 1 December 1905. Telegram, refuse to accept it at first, because of excess charges. But do so. A good thing too. B. informs me that I have been awarded the Nobel Prize.
> ... Sleepless night. Strange that it should bring me despondency instead of joy. But it is a splendid thing. Came to the decision not to travel to Christiana. Not up to it. Would probably suffer a breakdown in health.[26]

But she more than appreciated the advantages of a regular income : "It is nice to think that I have an assured income and will always be able to enjoy my creature comforts. Of course, if war and revolution come ... nothing is absolutely certain. Anyway, it has been a great stroke of fortune."[27] Although she was happy that she could now contemplate the prospect of old age without anxiety, it still pained her that this honour had not been bestowed upon her while her husband was still alive. "Silent and lonely tears for me, despite my Nobel Prize, a lonely old fool."[28]

NOTES

1. *Tagebuch*, 8 January 1897.
2. *Ibid.*, 9 January 1897.
3. *Ibid.*, 15 January 1897.
4. *Ibid.*, 26 October 1900.
5. *Memoiren*, p. 335.
6. *Tagebuch*, 13 February 1897.
7. *Ibid.*, 26 March 1897.
8. *Ibid.*, 8 January 1901.
9. H. Schück and R. Sohlmann, *Nobel—Dynamit, Petroleum, Pazifismus,* Paul List, Leipzig, 1928. Edition authorised by the Nobel foundation.
10. Nobel Archives, Nobel foundation, Stockholm. Letter from B. v. S. to A. N., 28 October 1895.

11. Library of the United Nations, Geneva, Peace archives, Collection Suttner-Fried, letter A. N. to B. v. S., 17 August 1885.
12. *Memoiren*, p. 271.
13. *Ibid.*, p. 271.
14. *Ibid.*, p. 270.
15. Cf Irwin Abrams, "Bertha von Suttner and the Nobel Peace Prize," *Journal of Central European Affairs*, October 1962.
16. *Tagebuch*, 15 May 1897.
17. *Ibid.*, 9 January 1897.
18. Nobel Archives, Nobel foundation, Stockholm. Letter from B. v. S. to A. N., 9 September 1892.
19. Nobel Archives, Letter from B. v. S. to A. N. 15 February 1893.
20. Nobel Archives, Letter from B. v. S. to A. N. 26 September 1895.
21. Melinite. Old explosive of French origin; no longer in production. Known in Britain under the name lyddite.
22. Nobel Archives, Letter from B. v. S. to A. N. 28 November 1896.
23. Library of the United Nations, Peace Archives, Collection Suttner-Fried, letter from B. v. S. 7 January 1893.
24. *Die Waffen nieder!* 1897, no. 4.
25. *Tagebuch*, 26 October 1900.
26. *Ibid.*, 1 December 1905.
27. *Ibid.*, 25 February 1906.
28. *Ibid.*, 14 January 1906.

THE DEATH OF ARTHUR SUTTNER

The last years before Arthur Suttner died were lived out in the shadow of financial worries. The Suttners had been obliged to work themselves to the limit in an attempt to save Harmannsdorf and maintain themselves and the family in the manner to which they were accustomed. They wrote a great deal, always working against time; there was no leisure for careful polishing of style and it was quite impossible for any pauses for creative thought. Like a nightmare the prospect of the final ruin of the family weighed upon Arthur Suttner and his wife day and night.

This was strain enough on her nervous resources, but there was another cause of emotional distress to her. A difference between her husband and herself threatened for a while to disrupt their life together, which had been so happy and harmonious. But it had largely been overcome well before his death. The cause of the tension between them was Arthur Suttner's not entirely avuncular interest in his niece Marie Luise von Suttner, the orphaned daughter of his eldest brother. All that the diaries from this period reveal—Bertha Suttner herself removed several pages from them—is that this niece had published a book, *Wie es Licht geworden.*[1] This book was a veiled account of her admiration for her uncle, but it was clear enough to those in the know. Nearly every day, Arthur Suttner would walk with Marie Luise in the park at Harmannsdorf, and this aroused Bertha Suttner's jealousy. Looked at with present-day eyes, the whole business seems trifling enough, little more than a psychologically interesting episode in the life of two people whose marriage would be considered happy and exemplary. Despite the fact that Arthur Suttner loved and respected his wife greatly, she cannot always have been an easy person to live with. She herself describes the strict, almost military, division of the day's work in Harmannsdorf, their work in their shared study, reading together, and so on. Little wonder that as a sensitive writer and the husband of a famous and extremely active woman, Arthur sometimes preferred the park to forced labour indoors and enjoyed chatting to his young and beautiful niece. On the other side of the coin, Bertha Suttner's jealousy is more than understandable. She was quite honest with herself and cherished no delusions about her appearance. She was clearly aware at that time of the great age difference that separated them, even though she did not want to express it openly, and this recognition must have depressed her not a little.

But the episode remained an episode; it passed, and its importance should not be exaggerated. But it does show Bertha Suttner in a human and, for once, a not so victorious light. Arthur Suttner's serious illness, which first made itself apparent early in 1902 and compelled her to travel alone to the peace congress in Monaco in April of that year, caused her to forget her jealousy and other cares. In the closing months of his life, which the couple spent partly in Harmannsdorf, partly in Abbazia, she was entirely the loving and devoted wife. Arthur Suttner's death in December 1902 was the greatest blow of her entire life. It marked the beginning of complete isolation, for their marriage had been childless. Never again did she regain her carefree joie de vivre and her delight in work which the knowledge of her own vigour used to give her. It was a cruel blow from which she never quite recovered. In the years immediately following on his death her love for him developed into a cult, from which her book *Letters to a departed Man*— proof to herself and others of her devotion and love—offered some release.

In accordance with a mutual promise they had made, she fulfilled his wish by having him cremated, not buried. Since at that time there was no crematorium in Vienna, Arthur Suttner's body was transported to Gotha, and there are macabre romantic overtones in Bertha Suttner's description in her diaries of how she and her husband's closest relatives ventured forth into the snow-covered park at Harmannsdorf on a chill winter's night and buried the urn at one of the deceased's favourite spots. This had caused quite an uproar among friends and relations of the Suttner family and provoked a great deal of criticism, for it was an entirely Catholic family. But the arrangement was in full accordance with the philosophy of life which Arthur and Bertha Suttner had already come to accept in their Caucasus days.

Under the influence of the philosophical and scientific studies which they had undertaken during their voluntary exile they had freed themselves from orthodox religious faith, and Bertha Suttner openly admitted this in her first popular non-fiction book about her convictions, *Inventory of a Soul*. "I can no longer conceive of him . . . and because we do not venture to name, nor describe, nor comprehend Him, people accuse us of atheism."[2]— "So it is not pride, not arrogance, nor the bravado of the devil for one to say of God : 'I cannot conceive of Him', but humility, profound, sincere humility."[3]—"Do not call us poor and unhappy because we do not look forward to any heaven. For nor do we have any fear of hell. We find such peace, such contented, happy clarity in our philosophy, that no one who has tasted of the tree of this knowledge can ever cease tasting."[4] Bertha Suttner also seeks to define her views on God in her book *Chess of Suffering*, which was completed in 1897 and contains many autobiographical details.

> By "God" I simply understand the divinity within the human breast. I know of no other—for to believe what men have said and written to us about it, is not to believe in God but in man. . . . But deep within glows a spark of the universal flame which kindled all the suns in the cosmos, there too can be heard an echo of the universal voice that uttered the words of a creation that is still continuing—and there too is the God who reveals himself to us.[5]

NOTES

1. Pierson, Dresden, 1898.
2. *Inventarium einer Seele,* Leipzig, 1883, p. 331.
3. *Ibid.,* p. 332.
4. *Ibid.,* p. 383.
5. *Schach der Qual,* p. 21.

THE PATH TO INDEPENDENCE

Her intensely subjective experience of God offered her no hope of reunion with her husband beyond the grave. In her later years she now and then experienced something approaching envy towards those able to draw such consolation from the Christian religion. When the feeling of loneliness oppressed her too greatly she longed for death, for oblivion, to be swept up into the void, into "Nirvana".

But life went on and continued to present Bertha Suttner with new challenges and to make new demands on her. After Arthur Suttner had passed away, there was a threat that family life in Harmannsdorf, which only held together with some difficulty, would break up entirely. Financial ruin was no longer to be averted. "I can see the collapse coming, and it causes me all manner of torment. Harmannsdorf is an organism that has long since been destroyed . . . it is a 'gouffre', on which all are bleeding to death."[1]—"The 'clef de voûte' has fallen in, and now the rest will collapse".[2]—"With Arthur's death the main beam has given way",[3] she laments in her diaries. She suffered greatly because of the family's circumstances, felt herself a prisoner, hemmed in, oppressed by the hopelessness of the situation.

It soon became clear to her that she would not be able to carry on working in such an atmosphere and under such circumstances. And she certainly had to work if she wanted to meet her obligations and to fulfil her husband's last wish as expressed in his will :

> You know that we have felt it our duty to do our bit towards improving the lot of the world, to work and fight for the good, for the undying light of truth. When I go, it does not mean that you are released from that obligation. . . . You must work on in the same spirit, continue working for our good cause until you too come to the end of life's journey. So be of good heart, do not be despondent. We are agreed about what we have achieved, so work on that still more might be achieved ![4]

So at the end of January 1903 she went to Vienna to make a short stay there. She resumed her work as lady president of the Peace Society, visited friends, and when she was alone again in her hotel bedroom she wrote, or wept over her loss. She was now reconciled with her niece Marie Luise "whom my dear husband loved so much, and who is after all my nearest relative now, however much she may have hated and persecuted me";[5] and the two of them often discussed the possibility of settling down in Vienna and trying to save the family possessions in Harrmansdorf.

She was now in her sixties but had lost none of her vitality, although she was well aware that the years that stretched before her would be lonely and without love, and that she would have to make all her own decisions and act entirely independently. This she found as hard to endure as the prospect of living alone and carrying on singlehanded the struggle which she and her husband had made into their life's work. She tried to accommodate her life to her changed circumstances. There were two experiences which helped to mitigate the suffering and despair of the first six months of widowhood: a friendship with Dr. Nussbaum, her husband's doctor in Abbazia, a relationship not without unmistakable erotic overtones, and her stay in Monaco as a guest of Prince Albert I.

This platonic flirtation with "Nussi", to whom she openly revealed her feelings, was a relationship she conducted consciously as a woman. It is true that she writes after a short visit by the doctor to Vienna at the beginning of the year: "Thus the sunset chapter is brought to an harmonious conclusion",[6] but it was not until July of the same year that she had completely recovered from the experience of this friendship. In her loneliness and isolation, she had revealed her whole emotional life in long detailed letters from Monaco to the charming doctor, but he—as her diaries reveal—had seen in her more a patient, spiritually isolated by the death of her husband, than an intimate friend.

She stayed in Monaco from 20 February to 26 March, and then returned home via Fiume and Abbazia. During her visit to the Adriatic resort she wrote:

A dear man who loves me—he will pluck the last blooms of life's flowers—but let there be no misunderstanding: it is a childlike love. When I read through these pages at some future date, I should not like the misunderstanding to arise that I forgot the dignity of my years, that I fell victim to the foolish notion that I could inspire other than innocent feelings. The most famous woman in all Europe—and a great lady—that should give some spice to the attachment, but also a touch of the novelette, a flash of passion.[7]

But just a few days later she confirms after reading "such a laboured, pedestrian and cold-hearted letter" directed to her that "I shall close the correspondence. The episode is over and done with. It's all finished."[8] It was not easy for her to renounce, because up until then she had been accustomed to succeed as a woman, to influence by her appearance and her imposing social presence. Her pride too was wounded, despite the fact that a survey conducted by an important German newspaper, the *Weltspiegel* (a supplement of the *Berliner Tageblatt*), on the five most famous women of the age had revealed that the public had given her the greatest number of votes, first place among women like Carmen Sylva, Sarah Bernhardt, Eleonore Duse and Marie v. Ebner-Eschenbach.

From this period on—"the sunset episode"—she began to write more and more in her diaries about the growing burdens of old age; she was an acute observer of herself and her effect upon the people around her, on the public in the course of a lecture or on the guests at a soirée. She lamented the loss of her old magnetism, and spoke sadly of her "anti-magnetism". She hated old women, they repelled her, and so she hated herself. In this "closing phase" of her life, she fought an embittered battle with herself. Doubtless a part of her longed for well-earned quiet and solitude. She was entranced by "the delights of nature, the young elder blossom, the scent of grass, the country," and she dreamed of the "shade of a tree of my own. . . . Nature is my passion, my last passion." She not infrequently entered into negotiations with agents, looked round country houses, signed contracts, and then cancelled them again. In 1914 she bought herself a country house in the southern part of Styria as a capital investment; her last journey took her to Rohitsch in order to inspect the property. More than once she considered giving notice on her Vienna flat; on one occasion she actually did so, but soon renewed the contract again. On the other hand, after months of hesitation, she turned down Count Heinrich Taaffe's offer to place at her disposal his castle in Bohemia, where she could retreat and spend the rest of her days.

She insisted that she would never accept any more official positions. But time and again she was swept along by the tide of events, and she was not really unhappy that this was so. According to her diary entries, she had always sought peace, nature, and time for her literary work, but these eluded her until the end.

Nor did the second episode of the first half of 1903 seem to have measured up to her expectations, although it had begun hopefully enough. At the beginning of the year she had received an invitation to the opening of the "Institut international de la Paix" in Monaco, which was under the patronage of Prince Albert I. According to the plans of its founder, this institute had the task of publishing works on international law, the peaceful resolution of international disputes, statistics on war and armaments, the development of international agencies and organisations, pacifist propaganda and pacifist instruction, as well as publicising the history and bibliography of pacifism. Prince Albert I, who was only a few years Bertha Suttner's junior, had served in the Spanish marine and had later devoted himself to the study of science. He was an oceanographer and writer who took an interest in the peace movement and was himself a pacifist. He had met Bertha Suttner on the occasion of the peace congress which gathered in Monaco in 1902. And now there came a personal invitation to her to come as his guest to his "castle on the rock", spend several weeks there and perhaps gain some diversion from her grief. "And Monaco itself can mean great things, even on an international plane", she noted. When she was still in Vienna she read his book *La Carrière d'un Navigateur*, an autobiographical work in which he openly declared his pacifist convictions, and she found him "a remarkable man".[9] And remarkable he certainly must have been. Contemporary opinion of him was as varied as it was in the case of Bertha Suttner herself, ranging from friendly favourable opinion of his work as an oceanographer to unpleasant remarks such as "somewhat mad, not normal".[10] His castle in Monaco was a meeting-place for the nobility and international pacifism. It was his dream to make his little city into the focal point of internationalism, as his secretary Gaston Moch once told Bertha Suttner.[11] Bertha Suttner doubtless rendered him great service by spreading harmony among his guests and bringing about closer relationships between members of the ruling houses and important members of the peace movement. He justified his invitation to her on the grounds that "my presence was beneficial and useful to him because of my influence with various people".[12] Prince Albert was also a friend of Wilhelm II and added a dedication to the Kaiser to the

German edition of his book. As far as can be gathered from Bertha Suttner's letters and diaries, he appears to have tried to influence him towards pacifism, and had even counted on his collaboration in a great demonstration in 1905 in which the "scientific and peace movement would be simultaneously publicised and celebrated". But the Kaiser just designed a peace banner for Albert, and a standard for the peace movement.

In Monaco Bertha Suttner was received with every honour; she had at her disposal a suite of rooms, a maid, a valet de pied and a carriage, and she revelled in the luxury that surrounded her. She felt contented and flattered at being the centre of attraction in the little city state. "I sit on his right hand and am served first."[13] On 25 February the opening ceremony of the "Institut de la Paix" took place, and in his speech the Prince referred to her in these terms: "We have the good fortune to have among us Bertha von Suttner, who is the moving spirit of the peace movement and its greatest advocate". He involved her in his literary work and in the translation of his book *La Carrière d'un Navigateur* into German. "He is very fond of that book. So I shall do the work a great service and thereby repay his hospitality."[14]—Albert's book must come out well."[15] She translated the book the Prince was so proud of with great enthusiasm and was very happy when the reviews were "magnificent" and quoted passages to prove how "beautifully" she really had translated it. She admired the prince, his youthfulness and his intelligence. "Yesterday, after my literary work, I gained the impression for a moment that I might come closer to Albert I, might become a person he needed. But in the evening the impression had vanished. I think he has had second thoughts, but we shall see."[16] As she describes a lady "who is supposed to be his lover", she feels a pang of jealousy. Whatever expectations she may have had from this visit, "it brought no miracles, but for all that it gave me precious memories".[17] Here too there is a note of resignation.

Having met any number of international figures, Bertha Suttner returned to Vienna after a stay lasting three weeks. She was pleased to report that one of the prince's guests, a Rothschild, had made a donation to the Peace Society in Vienna: "500 francs, which I am sending on to Vienna immediately. So my stay has not cost the society a penny".[18] She decided to go back to Harmannsdorf again, where she was awaited like "Providence", as she puts it.

Slowly she evolved the plan of living an independent life. "Although there is no lack of places where I can rest my head, I really shall have to have a home of my own."[19] On the return journey from Bern to Vienna, where she had travelled in May 1903 as vice-president of the Bern International Peace Bureau, she resolved to make a final break with Harmannsdorf and to set up house by herself. "That will give me a new lease of life and a secure base. To be at home, in my own house. To be independent, to work, to have roots in one place, where my possessions are."[20] She had her doubts as to whether she ought to carry out her plan before receiving the Nobel Prize. "Isn't it silly to settle down earlier! But I must have somewhere to call my own, and if I don't use my money to settle down it will gradually be frittered away."[21]

The thought of a home of her own cheered her up and she swept all doubt aside in this most characteristic statement: "I have always lived like that, and lived well and elegantly too. And I see no reason to change in this last brief stage of my life. Must keep earning."[22] And when she rented the flat in Vienna, Zedlitzgasse 7, she writes: "A strange thing, this new turn of events. I have taken an apartment. So the last stage of my life is turning out quite differently after all. But it can only be carried through if I work and earn my keep."[23]

The years that follow are characterised by that phrase "work and earn", even after she had received the Nobel Prize. All her actions, undertakings, lecture tours and literary activities can be explained in terms of the same principle: to work for the idea, to work and earn in order to be able to live well and in style.

NOTES

1. *Tagebuch*, 22 December 1902.
2. *Ibid.*, 30 December 1902.
3. *Ibid.*, 14 January 1903.
4. *Memoiren*, p. 539.
5. *Tagebuch*, 19 April 1903
6. *Ibid.*, 4 February 1903.
7. *Ibid.*, 28 March 1903.
8. *Ibid.*, 6 April 1903.
9. *Ibid.*, 22 January 1903.
10. *Ibid.*, 9 November 1911.
11. Library of the United Nations, Geneva, Peace Archives, Collection Suttner-Fried. Letter from G. Moch to B. v. S. 8 January 1902 (Jx 1–25).
12. *Tagebuch*, 11 April 1905.
13. *Ibid.*, 25 February 1903.
14. *Ibid.*, 16 March 1903.
15. *Ibid.*, 3 March 1903.
16. *Ibid.*, 24 February 1903.

17. *Ibid.*, 25 March 1903.
18. *Ibid.*, 24 March 1903.
19. *Ibid.*, 13 May 1903.
20. *Ibid.*, 2 June 1903.
21. *Ibid.*, 10 June 1903.
22. *Ibid.*, 27 June 1903.
23. *Ibid.*, 11 July 1903.

LITERARY ACTIVITIES

By work Bertha Suttner meant first and foremost to be active as a writer, to compose novels and short stories. But the growth and decline not only of her productivity, but also her popularity, can be traced in the pages of Hinrich's half-yearly calendar of the German book trade for the years 1881–1914 which span her literary activity; Hinrich reveals how industriously her first publishers, and later E. Pierson in Dresden and finally the Berlin-Vienna publishing company turned out book after book by their authoress. Publishing activity was particularly intense in the years up to 1905; after 1906, that is, after she had received the Nobel Prize, the numbers gradually decreased, and a temporary end came with her death and the outbreak of the First World War, when another popular impression of *Lay down your Arms* came out (191st–210th thousand) under the Berlin-Vienna imprint, as did a translation of the novel into Esperanto. No further impressions of the popular edition appeared until 1919. One of her first books, *Inventory of a Soul*, went into its fourth edition in 1904; and in the following year E. Pierson published a twelve-volume complete edition of her works. Her other novels and writings were also published in many editions so that, in the words of her Dresden publisher, they should always be available on sale.

Her last works did not appear under the Pierson imprint. *Voices and Figures*, a collection of essays that had been written some time before, was published by Elischer in Leipzig in 1907, her memoirs by the Deutsche Verlagsanstalt in Stuttgart in 1908, which had already published some of her husband's novels, and her last novel, *Man's noblest Thought*, appeared in the Friedens-Warte press in 1911.

The considerable successes as a writer which Bertha Suttner was still achieving in 1903 encouraged her in the belief that the publication of a novel would help her out of the long-standing series of financial crises in which she found herself. But first she wanted to produce "a worthy monument" to her husband. On her twenty-seventh wedding anniversary, in June 1903, she started work on the *Letters to a departed Man*, which contains an account of the last months of his life, his sufferings and his death, and bear witness to her love for her deceased husband. She hoped that by formulating such themes in an artistic framework she would write herself free of the pain in her soul and shrug off the weighty burden of grief. "However terrible its subject, art has always had this liberating, this satisfying quality."[1] Her little book appeared in 1904 and was reissued in the following year (4th–6th impression). Like *Es Löwos*, it recounts the most private details of her life and is, as she had intended, a "monument" after her own fashion. These letters could also be regarded as a defence of her marriage in the face of all those ill-wishers who disapproved of her relationship with a man so many years her junior. There was no justification in their attitude : the letters from Arthur Suttner which have been preserved are all couched in the warmest tones; more than once he expresses his gratitude for her love which had brought his life so much richness and happiness. So these *Letters to a departed Man* were regarded as a demonstration of mutual affection. As a book, it is of no great literary merit.

Her *Memoirs* are recounted in a far more interesting fashion, and even today they are still fresh and alive. It is a pity that they are only complete to the year 1902. She had planned to produce further volumes after her complete retirement from public life. But she was not able to carry out this plan. She fell in with the wishes of her friends, and "offered peace propaganda in the grand style"[2] to the world again, as she put it. When she was working on her memoirs she made use of old documents and diaries, the latter of which she then mostly burned, that is, those up to 1897, made selections and was surprised herself at the out of the ordinary, varied and exceptional account of her life she was able to unfold to her readers. It really did turn out to be a "gripping, valuable book—a real legacy".[3] Until the beginning of her political activities her mode of existence had been that of an extravagant woman who even in her youth had led the hardly mundane life of an Austrian countess. Her description of her experiences in the various European cities, the people she met and her nine-year residence in the Caucasus are much more fascinating and far more interesting to the present-day reader than any of her novels. Everything she describes bears the stamp of immediate experience, and this is the source of their direct impact on the reader. The development of the peace movement, the various congresses and the many personalities with whom the Suttners worked are all described in the most vivid manner, and a picture emerges of a world which for all its historical truth is not without a touch of unreality. For it is strangely moving to read of topics and issues which were then the centre of interest, and which even now are live issues which have yet to be resolved, like the United Nations, a federation of European states, Pan-Americanism, disarmament, war in the air, and many more. But at that time every campaigner was brimming with optimism, with faith in a better and brighter future, which men today, their idealism dulled by so many horrors, find almost inconceivable yet moving and almost shaming. The confidence of that generation of idealists in the rationality of man, their faith in the onward march of civilisation and the ultimate victory of the good have a shattering effect on the present-day reader. How differently the history of the last decades has turned out to be from the expectations of those apostles of peace, the idealists, pacifists and utopians! Of course they knew there would always be setbacks, they feared the outbreak of war, and did not believe that the efforts of their generation alone would be sufficient to wipe out the fundamental evil of war. They had their feet firmly planted on the ground, and in their mind's eye they had foreseen the disaster of the 1914–18 war, even the apocalyptic catastrophe of World War Two, but they did not believe that they would really happen. This attitude of theirs explains the wide gulf between them and the professional diplomats who at the time sought to dismiss such daydreamers with scornful laughter. None the less the ideas of these idealists advanced in parallel with the work of the professional politicians and diplomats and finally achieved some measure of success. Those who had begun by scorning often ended up by defending or even representing institutions which were either based on the principles of pacifism or developments of the pacifist idea, for example, the Interparliamentary Union, the League of Nations, the United Nations.

It is a matter for great regret that Bertha Suttner did not also include her later years in her memoirs; for this "closing phase of my life" was filled with such important events as the awarding of the Nobel Prize, her great lecture tours through Germany and the United States, in addition to her continuing activities as a journalist. All representations of her life, all the dramatisations, novels or films based on her adventurous career, depend on these memoirs and only offer an imprecise, lightly fantastical and inaccurate picture of the last years of her life.

As soon as they were translated into English, her memoirs became a great success in England and especially in the United States.

> And yesterday I had a nice letter about the memoirs from Stead. He writes about them in the *Review of Reviews* and calls Jane Addams and me "two of the greatest women in the world." My memoirs are now beginning to operate in my favour, but one is never a prophet in one's own land.[4]

She was encouraged by this response, and planned new literary ventures, although she was well aware of the fact that as a woman of letters she was no longer popular and "modern". Modern literature eludes me : I am still a Rossini . . . and I ought to be a Richard Strauss."[5]—"*Die neue Rundschau* seems to be going the same way."[6] But she still hoped that she might be able to make a go of literature once more, and was encouraged by the new fame which her memoirs had brought her to seek success in the field of the novel. *Man's noblest Thought* was begun on 6 September 1909 and work continued on it until 2 June 1910. On the day which she started she wrote optimistically in her diaries : "The first lines of my novel—reorganisation of Austrian society planned. So a little courage and endurance and the year 1910 could bring me a mention in the hall of fame. Possibly it will be my last word."[7] She was a realist and concerned with money matters and continued to operate on the principle of "work and earn in order to be able to live in style", as a later entry shows, ". . . and also brings in a good enough income, which is not to be laughed at (11,000 Kroner). I use up two pencils a day, and in June I shall have finished. I am sure that I am more than equal to the task."[8] But soon after, on 8 November, she was complaining : "Dead end. Writing is not so easy. But I must, I really must."[9] And later still : "It is a difficult gestation—for my novel just hasn't got any living characters. I cannot see their fate before me. The main theme was racialism, but that vein is exhausted. Where can I find living material for another two hundred pages? But I must, I must."[10]—"And one dead end succeeds another."[11] But her tone changed as the manuscript was nearing completion : "I am happy with the love chapter, and I think that after all it will be a good book."[12] And finally, on 2 June 1910, she writes : "At one o'clock in the morning I bring the manuscript of the book to a close with the blessed word 'Finis'."[13]

Bertha Suttner was a disciplined writer who worked to a strict routine, and she had finished the task which she had set herself; as planned, the completed manuscript lay before her in June. But was it the work of art which she hoped for and expected? Was the theme of the book the reorganisation of Austrian society as she had stated in her diary on 6 September 1909? No, she fell far short of her target. She certainly criticised, caricatured almost, Austrian nobility, as she did in all her novels, but her critique could never have brought about a reorganisation of society; in this literary form she was out of date in 1911. She herself admits that her novel lacks "living characters", and this observation holds good for all the figures she created. Her last novel was just one more in which she failed in her depiction of human beings. She admired Schnitzler and Thomas Mann, she read Bahr and the French moderns, but she could not match their achievement. But in the last analysis Bertha Suttner was not primarily concerned with man and his soul but with the illumination of those problems which preoccupied her at the time of writing, which were dear to her heart, and she often went about this in an exceedingly naïve, conventional and even banal fashion. But there are also sentences and paragraphs which betray the full range of her knowledge and personality. She puts her ideas across and draws projections of the future in a manner which truly reveal the logic and clarity of her mind.

As this is her last novel, it deserves some attention. The idea on which it is based puts forward a project which irresistably calls to mind Frank Buchman and Moral Rearmament which he founded, whose European centre is situated in Switzerland, in Caux. An enormously rich American—here Bertha Suttner is presumably taking Carnegie as her model—invites in the summer of every year some of the most important personalities in the worlds of science, art and politics to be his guests in Lucerne. Each has to undertake to give a lecture on his own field of work, and each lecture is disseminated in the press and by all other possible means. In this way, the enlightenment and education of millions of people can be enlisted to prevent the outbreak of war and a consequent decline into barbarity. No means should be spared in seeking to achieve the goal of preventing war, and no description of war waged with the new weapons can be horrific enough. As a true daughter of the nineteenth century, Bertha Suttner is fascinated by all the achievements of technology and by the hectic pace of technological progress. She was intensely interested in the possibilities opened by research into radium, possibilities of further advance or terrible destruction. Her imagination ran on :

> It is child's play to destroy enemy fleets in a few minutes by means of pulses of radium radiation transmitted from cloud-height. And both sides can do this. Forty-eight hours after the so-called "outbreak of hostilities" each of the warring nations can have defeated the other, leaving no one alive and not a single building standing in enemy territory.

Having thus described war in terms which foretell the atomic bomb, she continues with this appeal : "It is up to your will to decide whether or not to take the side of destruction."[14]

Bertha Suttner is no less fascinated by the conquest of the air which in the years before the First World War appeared to the public at large as an almost unbelievable miracle. But Bertha Suttner's fascination was matched by her fear of the dangers which could threaten mankind in the event of a war waged with these flying machines :

> Persecution, enslavement, deprivation of rights and mass destruction can no longer be regarded as acceptable means towards the attainment of social and political ends. For the possibilities of destruction have grown too great. The only way of protecting oneself against man in the air is to become that man's brother. We are standing at the crossroads—we can either rise up high, or sink into the abyss.[15]

Bertha Suttner ought have foreseen that prophecies of doom like these, especially couched in a scarcely modern and not very artistic form, would hardly be published willingly by any publisher, especially in times of intensive rearmament and of artificially inflamed nationalism. And indeed the manuscript did not find an outside publisher. Naturally enough, she offered it first to the Deutsche Verlagsanstalt, which, she wrote, she had up to then regarded as something of an exception among publishers. But she had been too hasty in making this observation in her diary. The very next day the manuscript was returned, and instead of a "guaranteed 10,000 Marks and a Christmas publication date" all she had was a manuscript "in the rascally hands of the publisher".[16] But she did not let herself be beaten that easily. The editor-in-chief of the Neue Freie Presse, Moritz Benedikt, was asked if he would like to view the manuscript. The Berlin-Vienna firm also read it, but neither accepted it. So she sent it on to Elischer in Leipzig, where her *Voices and Figures* had appeared in 1907. "Elischer too have sent the novel back to me. Where next? This is a sad old business. But I still believe I shall make it in the end."[17] But she found the going difficult. The *Neues Wiener Tageblatt* rejected it unread. "Doesn't my name mean anything, then?"[18]—"Fischer has turned it down—why are they all so unanimous? Am I a nobody?"[19]—"Westermann said no because it was too political."[20]—"Diederich because it lacks realism—the generation gap. In other words, I have become old-fashioned." But she had become hardened in the long years of struggle. "I do not believe it. They only suspect it to be so, because I am old."[21] But a few days later another refusal comes. "Langen turns me down." For the first time she begins to have her doubts:

> Is my novel really bad? I am almost beginning to believe it myself. It does lack a sense of reality. A pity. Now it's off to Machold. I don't hold out any hopes from that quarter. The real culprit is my name, which is a dead letter as far as literature is concerned. It has no market value. In the eyes of the public the pacifist has slain the authoress. Pacifism is the stronger title and will be of greater benefit for generations to come. Still it is a blow and I feel it as such.[22]

After this run of failures Fried came to the rescue. In October 1911 the novel appeared under the Friedens-Warte imprint, subsidised by good friends from abroad; and in November of the same year she records happily "900 copies disposed of already",[23] and the beginning of December "over 1,000 sold".[24]

Despite favourable reviews in the pacifist journals, the book gained no success. It really had been an unexpected blow to Bertha Suttner to find the manuscript rejected by so many publishers, all the more so because her earlier novels had sold well and *Lay down your Arms* had been one of the most sensationally successful books of the turn of the century. But Bertha Suttner had indeed become old-fashioned, an outmoded authoress. In her own lifetime she experienced at first hand what it was like to be rejected by publishers and public alike and to suffer the lot of the committed writer whose gifts are not great enough to express views in a form viable on its artistic merits alone. In 1913 the idea appears in her diaries again of writing another novel, or of dramatising *Man's noblest Thought*—a completely crazy notion. She was not enough of an artist to achieve universality, she herself must have had doubts about the practicality of such projects. For she had really ceased to be a writer back in 1911.

Her dream of working as a novelist in quiet seclusion was over
and gone. But it is questionable whether she would ever have been
content to live far from society life and the bustle of political
activity.

NOTES

1. *Tagebuch,* 16 July 1903.
2. *Ibid.,* 12 October 1906.
3. *Ibid.,* 8 November 1907.
4. *Ibid.,* 8 February 1910.
5. *Ibid.,* 10 October 1906.
6. *Ibid.,* 10 October 1906.
7. *Ibid.,* 6 September 1909.
8. *Ibid.,* 15 September 1909.
9. *Ibid.,* 8 November 1909.
10. *Ibid.,* 12 January 1910.
11. *Ibid.,* 28 January 1910.
12. *Ibid.,* 25 May 1910.
13. *Ibid.,* 2 June 1910.
14. *Der Menschheit Hochgedanken,* Berlin, 1911, p. 395.
15. *Ibid.,* p. 295.
16. *Tagebuch,* 5 August 1910.
17. *Ibid.,* 23 October 1910.
18. *Ibid.,* 27 January 1911.
19. *Ibid.,* 15 February 1911.
20. *Ibid.,* 19 May 1911.
21. *Ibid.,* 16 July 1911.
22. *Ibid.,* 28 July 1911.
23. *Ibid.,* 16 November 1911.
24. *Ibid.,* 2 December 1911.

"LIVING IN STYLE"

In the "closing phase of my life," in which she felt so lonely and rejected, she liked to cultivate her social contacts and lead a life in society. It was not uncommon for her to attend several "at homes" on the same afternoon and to record contentedly in her diary: "In the evening I deck myself out in my silken finery and take myself off to Goluchowski and am thoroughly fêted. Almost a court reception."[1] Or again: "Déjeuner chez Lubomirska, which makes me feel more fashionable."[2] But a month later she is complaining that she finds "no more pleasure in socialising in high society,"[3] but does find a soirée at Count M.'s, where she had been taken by a Count Resseguier, to be "interesting." Even in 1909 she was sprightly enough to join a luncheon party with her friends Count and Countess Taaffe (she notes precisely that twelve were present), played bridge there until six in the evening and took supper at another gathering elsewhere, again making an exact record of the number of guests (twenty on this occasion). And in 1911 she was writing:

> In the evening I make the effort and go to the Redlich household. Once there, I forget my tiredness and am quite lively. Among those present: Professor Jodl, Weingartner with Lucille Marcel, Marie Renard, Rosa Papier, Schmedes, Stefan Zweig, Rosé, etc. Splendid piece for orchestra by Weingartner (fourth symphony). Much charm from Lucille. Between Weingartner and Jodl at supper (lavish). After supper more music (which gets a little too much). Back home at one thirty.[4]

Despite all the progressiveness, modernity and equality among men she was not insensitive towards the attitude of the nobility. A luncheon at Prince Kinsky's palace was followed by a cultural tour of the building. "After all, there is something in feudal splendour. Understandable that they are conservative."[5] She was also enchanted with the magnificence of the Kolovrat palace.

For Christmas or Easter she liked to go to Stockern, an estate in Lower Austria, in order to spend the holiday period with her brother-in-law's family. Count and Countess Taaffe were the most popular among the friends who often invited her, and the days she spent in a castle in Bohemia which belonged to the count, were among her most peaceful times.

But there were some members of the Austrian aristocracy, that most conservative of classes, who gave Bertha Suttner a wide berth. Even today there are some people who become extremely reticent at the mention of her name and recall that "Bertha was not one of our circle, she was so eccentric". An experience Bertha Suttner had during a stay by the Wörthersee in the summer of 1904 offers a typical instance of this attitude. It had been a summer of much work, but also of considerable success for her. Several articles had appeared in a variety of papers and the details for her journey to the USA settled. She noted in her diary that "Boston is happy with all the arrangements," and then records with a blend of surprise and a mild sense of shock : "On the journey back (by steamer) an encounter with aristocratic company, who were talking about Bertha Suttner. I made myself known. All I received by way of answer was 'Really?' "[6]

Bertha Suttner had had the courage to leave her own confined circle and to go her own way outside the terms of reference of her own class and the society to which she belonged by birth and upbringing, in order to advocate and defend ideas totally foreign to the traditions of her caste. She was aware of the vast gulf that separated her from those who were either unwilling or unable to understand her. After a visit by relations of her husband's family she wrote : "Have just about nothing in common with this 'coterie' nor they with me. They think I'm something of a joke."[7] On another occasion she wrote : "Dropped by to see Margarethe. She was just dressing for dinner. Told me about her night life. It seems so trite to me. She knows nothing about what is going on in the world outside : the English miners' strike."[8] And while she was staying at a friend's country residence one summer she complained bitterly :

M. doesn't show the least interest in my cause. Doesn't even read the *Friedens-Warte* given to her. I see in this present environment the kind of wall of incomprehension and indifference that those who seek change have to contend with. We are treated as mad or at the very least as nuisances. We are a nuisance because we represent a threat to the peace of the status quo in which they have their comfortable niche. Because they are members of the establishment, they are aware of its power to resist change. But they know nothing of the might of the cause of progress—and haven't the least notion of what has already taken place. In Russia, and particularly in Poland—outbreaks of murder, persecution of the Jews,, one has already got quite hardened to them. Revolution is already upon us, and the world at large is still asking itself : "Is it suppressed or overwhelming us?"[9]

The hours she spent with artists and writers marked a stimulating and enjoyable contrast. Her brief comments bring alive the life style and atmosphere of the intellectual and rather snobbish society of pre-1914 Vienna. They tell of her visits to Lilli Lehmann, with whom she was on the most cordial and intimate of terms, or a visit to the "Bahr-castle" in Ober-St. Veit, which "is so hard to find" and of which she writes happily : "A few interesting hours spent there : poets and tragedies in song—that makes a scintillating pair."[10] She also gives a graphic description of a visit to Arthur Trebitsch :

Sunday. Trebitsch fetches me in the automobile. Pleasant conversation during the journey. About Shaw . . . and also my new novel. Arrival at the house. Splendidly furnished (modern style, of course, somewhat lacking in beauty of line). First Professor Gregori—a pretty, elegant young woman. A walk in the garden. Viewing the house with its library, billiard room, bathrooms, dressing rooms, studies, and guest rooms. Paul Zifferer and Raoul Auernheimer as guests. Conversation a delight. Zifferer an attractive homme du monde. Fluent French. Tells about Don Jaime. Wrote the manifesto for him. Jaime horrified at the Czar's cowardly gruesomeness—or rather, the other way round : gruesome cowardliness. Over coffee in the library the conversation exclusively on literary themes : Hauptmann the greatest writer. . . . Hermann Bahr on Herzl.—Back home on the tramcar. It was delightful. Real sociability. And such charming domesticity. If only my husband and I had such a home ! In the evening I am sleepy, and neglect my duties.[11]

Or : "An interesting afternoon with the Schnitzlers. His wife is also of a high intellect. He is most witty. Says he is a reader of the *Friedens-Warte*. Agrees with its aims, but believes it will be 100,000 years before they are realised."[12] Or again : "In the evening Herzl celebration—interesting conversations with Salten and H. Bahr."[13] Or again : "Tea in the Bristol Hotel. All the intelligentsia in Vienna present. In the evening 'musique' in the Japanese embassy."[14] As late as 1908 she was still going to the Concordia ball, as the guest of her literary and journalistic friends.

As far as her diaries reveal, she did not put on many social events herself. She had her "at home" day, but, dearly as she would have liked to, she did not succeed in leading a "salon" of her own, the main reason being that she did not really have the gift of accommodating herself to others, and besides, she did not have the time for this kind of socialising. "Don't know how to go about forming a salon. I'd rather travel. A season in London, a season in Rome. And also a quiet home in the country."[15] Even in the autumn of 1913 she was planning to live "more fashionably", so that she could campaign in society for the world peace congress that was to take place in Vienna in 1914.

She enjoyed spending the evening in one of Vienna's theatres. There is no mention in her diaries of her visiting any of the big concerts. Her main love was operatic music, and she was an enthusiast for contemporary opera. Her enthusiasm for Richard Strauss and his *Elektra* caused her to have a sleepless night, and she fervently re-enacted the scenes of this opera to her loyal servant Kathi. She also went to see the most sensational operetta of those years—*The Merry Widow*—and found: "This Treumann as Danilo an erotic poison. The throngs that go to the operetta, a kind of mass hysteria."[16] She liked to go to the Burg-theater, the Volkstheater with Hansi Niese, whom she greatly admired, and the "Ronacher", and later she took an interest in the first film performances in the little Kruger cinema, always receptive to what was new and interesting. And this was the same woman who supposedly yearned for a solitary life in the country.

NOTES

1. *Tagebuch,* 13 September 1904.
2. *Ibid.,* 18 January, 1908.
3. *Ibid.,* 16 February 1908.
4. *Ibid.,* 15 December 1911.
5. *Ibid.,* 4 May 1907.
6. *Ibid.,* 13 August 1904.
7. *Ibid.,* 14 March 1905.
8. *Ibid.,* 5 March 1912.
9. *Ibid.,* 17 August 1906.
10. *Ibid.,* 4 November 1910.
11. *Ibid.,* 17 October 1909.
12. *Ibid.,* 29 October 1913.
13. *Ibid.,* 5 December 1908.
14. *Ibid.,* 4 April 1911.
15. *Ibid.,* 2 February 1906.
16. *Ibid.,* 27 October 1906.

THE AUSTRIAN PEACE SOCIETY

She also felt a continuing sense of obligation to the "Austrian Society for the Friends of Peace," whose founder she was and whose lady president she continued to be; she had represented the society at the annual world peace congresses and the society itself felt a growing need for her active participation in the years after 1899, the year of the peace conference in The Hague. For much had changed since the foundation of the society in 1891 and its enthusiastic beginnings. The well-known names who had represented it, such as Count Hoyos and Prince Wrede, had either died or retired like the interparliamentarian Baron Peter Pirquet. A band of willing supporters remained, but they lacked the ability to put the cause across, to operate on a journalistic plane; and they also lacked personality, the right kind of connexions, and also the opportunity to exert influence on a political or social level. Bertha Suttner had no illusions about the difference in intellectual quality that obtained between the leading figures of the peace movement abroad and the representatives of her own Vienna committee.

> Letter from Hex (Countess Hedwig Pötting, her best friend and secretary) about the pettiness of the Peace Society since the movement as a whole has grown so large. She is right. For a long time I have regarded the Austrian Peace Society as a rather wretched affair. And yet. . . .[1]

This state of affairs was not far short of tragic, and did not make her old age any more tolerable. "And how much still remains undone!" Among the younger generation of the friends of peace in Vienna there was no personality, or at least none emerged, like Masaryk, later to be President of the Czechoslovakian Republic. She saw many more capable personalities in the societies of other countries, and this made the waning of her own powers doubly burdensome to her. She was pained by the disintegration of the society, which was beyond repair since the root cause was the state of affairs in Austria, and she would have liked to "shake off" the society, because it was lethargic and moribund. Nor did she have a high regard for those who worked with her; she caustically entitled them the "twelve apostles" or her "Eumenides" or again her "sleeping partners", and accused them of doing nothing more than a great deal of "tub-thumping". Anyone looking through the reports of the monthly meetings of the society, which were published in *Die Friedens-Warte*, will see that they are mainly concerned with discussions about treaties, the distribution of papers and pamphlets, the drafting of letters of thanks to ministers, and the like. It is true that they managed to found new groups, like those in Linz and Marienbad, but these were hardly of fundamental significance for the international peace movement. They were accorded international recognition only because their president was no less a personality than Bertha Suttner. But she herself did not feel up to a lone battle against such mediocrity. "Afternoon meeting. Absolutely nothing concrete happens. Am no real president."[2] She was also far from content with the official representatives of Austria at the Interparliamentary Union and gave vent to this outburst: "Official Austrian pacifism is in a state like this and I am supposed to fight against it in my old age. It needs new blood. The old guard ... who bear the marks of failure won't get anywhere!"[3]

When she discovered that plans had been drawn up as part of the peace congress which was to take place in London in 1908 for audiences of the individual peace societies with King Edward VII, she was shaken out of her lethargy and despondency, for in her opinion none of the other leaders of her society was worthy to represent Vienna abroad. She wrote in horror: 'No, we can't let 'Hütchen' (nickname of a society member) go. The die is cast. I am going to London."[4] And she made ready for the journey with great enthusiasm, took part in all the activities in London, gave a speech in Queen's Hall, was flattered when it came to her ears that the Queen had expressed the wish to be present when the delegates were received so as to be able to meet Bertha Suttner. She tried to make new contacts and was dejected when a visit with Carnegie in Skibo castle did not produce more successes for the "cause". During this time in London she was once again her old self, the enthusiastic campaigner for the peace movement she had been in the early days.

Despite the success she had, she seriously intended to retire from her presidency of the Austrian Peace Society on her seventieth birthday. Her work for the society could be no source of great satisfaction for her, because she loved generosity, breadth, and the international scene; she was no friend of petty middle-class attitudes, and was certainly no committee type. And when Fried called "her society" a "tea circle" she heartily concurred.

NOTES

1. *Tagebuch*, 20 July 1906.
2. *Ibid.*, 9 March 1909.
3. *Ibid.*, 18 December 1911.
4. *Ibid.*, 11 June 1908.

BERTHA SUTTNER AND A. H. FRIED

Fried was also the only one of her Viennese peace friends whom she acknowledged all through the years of "the last stage of my life" as her collaborator and fellow campaigner. If he had not been in evidence, Bertha Suttner would scarcely have had a single friend of like persuasion who matched her intellectual gifts and offered the opportunity for discussions on the problems of pacifism.

The unknown young man, "all fire and flame", who had founded the German Peace Society in 1891 in Berlin and had edited the journal *Die Waffen nieder!* had now become an internationally recognised pacifist, publicist and journalist. He had committed all his energies to putting across the ideas and aspirations of the peace movement, and hundreds of articles from his pen had appeared in newspapers and periodicals. He was to be found at nearly all the peace congresses and interparliamentary conferences writing up reports for the German press. He was also engaged as a correspondent for various papers. From 1896 to 1900 he edited the *Monatliche Friedenskorrespondenz,* the monthly journal of the German Peace Society, in 1895 the *Annuaire de la Vie internationale,* in 1899 founded the *Friedens-Warte,* which was still being published in 1962 under the editorship of Hans Wehberg.[1] Later he sought to extend his activities on behalf of the peace movement by lecturing in Germany, Austro-Hungary and Switzerland. Measured by modern standards, his activities could be compared to those of a public relations officer. The Nobel Prize awarded to him in 1911 was a mark of recognition in the highest quarters of his dedication in the struggle against war and on behalf of the ideals of the peace movement.

During the First World War he had to leave Austria and Germany and emigrated to Switzerland, where he continued to campaign vigorously for his convictions. He firmly believed that a new world would emerge from the war, a world that had nothing in common with the old. "This First World War must inevitably lead to a genuine world peace." He saw his task and that of the peace movement as seeking to ensure that "no peace of the old kind emerges which simply parcels out land and settles on reparations, but a real peace which bases the relationships between states on a new, secure foundation".[2] But he was bitterly disappointed by the way the peace negotiations of 1918–19 turned out and the consequent peace treaty of Versailles. He wrote these embittered words :

> Parcelling out land and reparations yet again, once more dis- content and anarchy and in their train a prospect of renewed re- armament and a continuation of despotism. The conclusion of a peace that once more just ends a war without establishing a true state of peace which would mark the end of wars once and for all time.[3]

In 1920 he published a pamphlet entitled *Weltprotest gegen den Versailler Frieden*, which documents his bitter disappointment at the Versailles treaty. Shortly after, in 1921, he died in Vienna.

His publicity work and activities as a lecturer were principally restricted to German-speaking territories, whilst Bertha Suttner was also active abroad, because of her excellent knowledge of languages; she spoke and wrote English, French, and Italian. Thus she and Fried complemented one another in their areas of operation. They were fellow campaigners : both were propagandists, and both employed the same weapons of journalism and public speaking. Although separated by age and background, their relations were on a very comradely level. It was an honourable friendship. Despite frequent differences of opinion, which occasionally led to incivilities and hurtful frankness, they continued to pursue their common aims together. Fried admired Bertha Suttner as a brave aristocrat who had courageously entered the lists in the cause of the disputatious and much-scorned ideals of the peace movement. And she admired him as an uncompromising pacifist of outstanding intelligence. In the first years of their work together he was still her "disciple", but he soon became a campaigner on equal terms and not infrequently took the initiative in many questions and decisions, and often became her successor, while she was still alive, in various organisations. It is hardly surprising that this change in Fried caused tensions between two such marked personalities. Although Bertha Suttner was the first to recognise his competence and superiority, she often felt that he had deprived her of the limelight. For a woman like her, self-assured, accustomed to success, and "pretentious", as Professor Lammasch once dubbed her, it was not always easy to be pushed into the shade by a younger person. "Fried's manner is certainly a little aristocratic; I haven't completely abdicated yet."[4] She fought a vigorous rearguard campaign against his influence gaining the upper hand. But despite that she was far from discontent when he lavished praise upon her and stressed her vitality; and she let his decisions prevail, and placed great value on his approval in her enterprises, for example, her American lecture tour.

A few extracts from her diaries will serve to illustrate this running state of tension and her alternations of mood.

Afternoon Schuster and Fried. Now there is a wall between Fried and myself. It has arisen because of my symptoms of old age which have made me "récalcitrant" and caused him to lose confidence in me. The harmony has gone. And his views on The Hague are quite different. It is not nice of me not to assist him with the *Friedens-Warte* and *Popolo*. But I am so filled with anxiety for the future.[5]

Or: "There is something so unpleasant, so superior about Fried these days."[5] In 1908 the main point at issue was the proposal to hold a peace congress in Vienna in 1910 which Bertha Suttner opposed. "He wants the congress in Vienna in 1910—too much for me."[7] Their discussions must have been extremely violent. "No, I will not let myself be tyrannised like that."[8]—"No, I must drop the Vienna congress, I must not take it upon myself. It would be too much for me, and would be a ghastly fiasco. In this place—I have no prestige left at all."[9]

She took it as a matter of course that Fried should approach her for directives for Bern, for the International Bureau of the peace movement, but on the other hand it pained her to record that "he was invited to Monaco, but I was not. Ah well, I didn't really want to go."[10]

Fried was a tireless worker, and so he also demanded unceasing effort from Bertha Suttner. As she put it, he would crack "the whip", and spur a tiring Bertha Suttner on to ever new achievements and undertakings. "I am plagued by tasks I cannot fulfil."[11]—"Fried demands leading article by Thursday morning."[12] But she never failed to write her regular commentary on contemporary affairs for the *Friedens-Warte*; however difficult she found it, she would even break off conversation with friends and go off to write deep into the night in order to fulfil her obligations.

As they had no telephones, they corresponded, often more

than once in a single day, and if no letter arrived she would record sternly in her diaries: "This Fried is a strange fellow. Quite extraordinary. First he says the *Friedens-Warte* will be ready on Saturday, and now another two days have passed without news."[13] Or: "Fried is happy that I did not pass comment on the bitterness of his letter."[14] And a few days later: "Fried has written me a letter even more unpleasant than the last one. He is quite rude . . . I'll answer in detail."[15] Then again she records an unfavourable observation made by the interparliamentarians which Fried certainly did not let slip unintentionally; it concerned a banquet for Professor Lammasch presided over by Freiherr von Plener, president of the Austrian group of the Interparliamentary Union. Bertha Suttner had hoped to be invited to this banquet.

> But it rankles that I was passed over. As a "lady" I did not expect to be invited, because there were only gentlemen present, but as a holder of the Nobel Prize, as the founder of the Austrian group of the Union.[16]

Partly to console her, but partly too to act as a corrective against her somewhat excessively "pretentious" attitude, Fried explained the view of the gentlemen in authority.

> Visit by Fried. Told me how Plener turned down the idea of Bertha Suttner as a guest at the banquet: "You don't know how much that lady is feared, she would give offence to many people." Anyway, Fried will give a speech at the banquet on the Austrian peace movement and so will mention my name.[17]

Fried remained on the friendliest of terms with her for all his frankness, and was ever concerned not to hurt the feelings of an ageing lady. Harmony prevailed over the celebrations in 1911 of twenty years of collaboration, and even before Fried's Nobel Prize had become public knowledge, she was the first to hear of the award: "Another surprise. Fried came and threw himself at me.—I feared his wife had died.—But the 'bad news' was none other than: 'I have won the Nobel Prize!'"[18] Despite all the alarums and excursions, despite all the annoyances, differences of opinion, quarrels and reconciliations, the overriding impression of this collaboration between an old lady of the Austrian nobility and the enthusiastic, gifted, idealistic pacifist of Jewish origin is that of a close and sincere relationship which was not lacking in warmth. What they shared was a common enthusiasm for the cause of the peace movement to which they sacrificed their time and energies.

The entries in Bertha Suttner's diaries underline the true extent of the demands which other members of the peace movement imposed upon her. The more her name became internationally known the more her friends thought they should involve her in campaigning and propagandising on behalf of the movement. Her energies were repeatedly drained to the point of utter exhaustion, but whenever she sought a moment's pause for breath and relaxation they invoked her sense of duty. "Il faut remplir ses devoirs," was how her old friend Passy put it. Time and again in her diaries she complained of overwork, tiredness, the waning of her powers. Naturally, any success delighted her, and flattered her self-esteem; and there was more than a touch of vanity in her awareness of her growing international fame and recognition. "Received a letter from Peking today. I am known everywhere."[19]—"My reputation is working for me now."[20] Even as an old lady, she retained her youthful thirst for knowledge, and was always excited by the new and the unknown; she continued to attend the sessions of the International Peace Bureau in Bern and the annual world peace congresses until the end of her seventieth year in 1913. She also was present at the second peace conference in The Hague in 1907, and accepted many invitations to undertake lecture tours.

NOTES

1. Verlag für Recht und Gesetz, Basle. (The journal, then in its 56th volume, ceased publication in 1962.—Translator.)
2. A. H. Fried, *Der Weltprotest gegen den Versailler Frieden,* Leipzig, 1920, p. 5.
3. *Ibid.,* p. 5.
4. *Tagebuch,* 24 October 1913.
5. *Ibid.,* 13 December 1907.
6. *Ibid.,* 11 June 1908.
7. *Ibid.,* 2 February 1909.
8. *Ibid.,* 20 July 1909.
9. *Ibid.,* 22 April 1909
10. *Ibid.,* 3 March 1910.
11. *Ibid.,* 21 January 1904.
12. *Ibid.,* 5 September 1905.
13. *Ibid.,* 8 December 1913.
14. *Ibid.,* 3 March 1910.
15. *Ibid.,* 18 March 1910.
16. *Ibid.,* 27 November 1910.
17. *Ibid.,* 27 November 1910.
18. *Ibid.,* 9 December 1911.
19. *Ibid.,* 23 October 1906.
20. *Ibid.,* 28 August 1906

"NOTRE GÉNÉRAL EN CHEF"

The International Peace Bureau in Bern was the focal point of the peace movement, the headquarters of the peace societies, where the plan of campaign for the coming year and the general staff strategy for the battle against war were drawn up.

The Bureau was established on the basis of a motion put forward in Rome in 1891 by the Dane Frederik Bajer, the founder of the Danish peace societies and of the Scandinavian Inter-parliamentary Union. In his motion, Bajer had drawn attention to the fact that "uninterrupted contact must be maintained between all existing peace societies and any new ones that emerge. All these individual units working towards a common goal essentially form part of one single corporate body."[1]

The lack of channels of communication between the individual peace societies in the nineteenth century is due to the fact that they were founded quite independently of one another and moreover owed their origins to a whole variety of different philosophies. The founders of the first society in the USA were members of the Quaker sect, which had grown up in England in the seventeenth century and which regarded the struggle against war as one of their principal objectives. The first peace society was founded in New York in 1815, and others followed independently of the first in other states, but as early as 1828 they succeeded in setting up the American Society of Peace, which incorporated them all. The first London peace society was also brought into being by a Quaker. The first such group to appear on the continent, the Société de la Paix, founded in Geneva in 1830, also owed its existence to purely religious motives. The numerous other European peace societies, which had formed in the course of the succeeding decades in France, Belgium, Holland, Italy and Germany, took as their model either Hugo Grotius, or Immanuel Kant, or the Encyclopedists of the French Revolution, according to their nationality.

In the first congresses of the national societies, those of 1843, 1848, 1849 and 1850, which were the predecessors of the great world peace congresses, only England and the USA were represented at first. Not until later did other states join them, but even in these early gatherings attempts were made to test the political and economic Utopias of their great forebears against the realities of the nineteenth century. The real systematic work of the peace movement did not, however, get under way until the first world peace congress, which met in Paris in 1889 under the chairmanship of Frédéric Passy, an important political figure of the day. Ten countries were represented by ninety-seven participants.

The more national societies that came into being, the greater the need became for co-ordination. This was the task of the International Bureau in Bern, as was the organisation of the peace congresses and the subjects to be placed on their agenda. The Bern Bureau, as it was known for short, was a thorough and efficient organisation; in meeting after meeting every question was scrutinised with the greatest attention to detail, as the records and protocols in the archives of the library of the United Nations in Geneva demonstrate.

Soon after the Bureau had been founded in 1892 and Elie Ducommun took over the task of running it, Bertha Suttner was named its vice-president. This marked a recognition of her organisational abilities and brought her the title "notre général en chef", which Passy had bestowed on her when an old man, recognition too of her diplomatic acumen, her wide experience, and her tireless zeal in the struggle for the preservation of peace. Rarely was she absent from the discussions in Bern; and her position in the team of workers there can best be demonstrated by means of two letters. The first, which dates from 9 March 1893, comes from her pen and was written to Ducommun. In it, she vigorously expounds her views on a number of basic issues, and the reader will readily recognise that she more than deserved the title of "général en chef", and that it was more than just a courtesy rank given to her by the Frenchman Passy.

Dear friend and colleague,

I am in receipt of your open letter to the health conference and I hope that it will appear in the issue for the twelfth. It is a miniature masterpiece. It says everything that has to be said in the most succinct language. I hope that it will do our cause yet another distinguished service.

I admire you and the way in which you have handled all the delicate questions the Bureau has put forward. It is my hope that the notion of "nationalities" will be done away with once and for all. There is less danger in the question itself than in the foolish, touchy and laughable individuals who raise it; our gatherings will not gain in credibility until these people leave our ranks. Every developing organisation owes its growth not only to the valuable elements which help it to flourish, but also to the strength of character to weed out harmful elements.

Have you seen the enclosed article from the *Diplomaten-Kurier*—a pretty miserable pacifist paper? The article is bad but it does reveal the Achilles' heel of our congresses: it demonstrates the dangers we are exposing ourselves to if we permit national, religious and other discussions to obtrude into our work. Such matters are divisive—and even worse, they exclude us from contact with many who stand outside our movement but wish to join it.

But we shall march onward! The news that Mr. Gobat had passed on to me about the formation of a parliamentary party in Pest is a great step forward in the right direction. Now we shall be able to found a sister society in Hungary.[2]

The second letter is by Albert Gobat himself, the director of the International Peace Bureau and successor to Ducommuns. It is dated 6 June 1913 and offers Bertha Suttner congratulations on her seventieth birthday, thanks her for the work she has done for the organisation and informs her that she has been accorded the title of Honorary President. Gobat's words reveal profound respect for her twenty years of tireless work for the peace movement:

You have aroused those sentiments of humanity which all too often have not proven sufficiently strong to defend themselves successfully at a time when it is a sacred duty to take a stand against force. You cried out "Lay down your arms!" in order to proclaim the fact that man is not a mere creature at the mercy of savage, unrestrained drives, but the creator of justice. Under the influence of your warm-hearted words a great army has grown up which recoils from the shameful and blasphemous assertion of the politicians that "might is right." They have thronged about the banner which you so honourably have held up on high. At your calling, numerous peace societies came into being. Your name is among those who have advanced the work of the International Peace Bureau, whose Vice-President you have been, and whose Honorary President you now are.[3]

Thus another chapter in her strenuous life came to an end, a life which she lived to the full and from which she gained great richness and meaning through her idealism.

NOTES

1. *Die Waffen nieder!* 1892, no. 4.
2. Library of the United Nations, Geneva, International Peace Bureau, meetings, 1892–1895 (IF).
3. Library of the United Nations, Geneva, Peace archives, Collection Suttner-Fried (Fe II/14).

"CONCILIATRIX"

If the Bern Bureau was the head office of the societies where their work was co-ordinated, the congresses marked a show of strength, visible proof of the international standing of the peace movement. Bertha Suttner revelled in the atmosphere of these international congresses, and the bustle of these gatherings re-charged her spiritual strength and gave her renewed vigour. She took part in nearly every congress from the third world peace congress in Rome 1891—where she attended as the lady presi-dent of the then newly-founded Austrian Peace Society, gave a public speech for the first time in her life and was accepted by all those present as an equal in the campaign for peace—right up until 1913; the only ones she missed were the fifth (Chicago 1893), tenth (Glasgow 1901), eighteenth (Stockholm 1910), and the nineteenth (Geneva 1912). She also attended the majority of the interparliamentary conferences, unofficially, as their guest. It is true that in the years immediately before her death it was her intention to keep away from all public functions, to reject all invitations and leave the way open for others, because she felt too old to make public appearances, and too tired and weak to take upon herself all the burdens of conferences and discussions, speeches and receptions—but at the eleventh hour, the last pos-sible moment, she would change her mind about going off to London, Munich or Milan, or wherever the congress was being held. It "was to be". She would always find some compelling reason for going which was at the same time a self-justification : it was her "sense of duty", she claimed, that compelled her presence at these congresses. In her diaries she writes after nearly every journey : "That was my last congress," and yet the very next year she was off again, taking part in all the discussions, giving speeches herself, deeply offended if she was held to be tired, old or sick, and recording with satisfaction whenever she was given a good place at table at the big official dinners and when a lot of people had introduced themselves to her in the course of the various functions.

What was Bertha Suttner's real role at these congresses? She was not a practising politician, nor was she a member of any parliament, a legal expert or a diplomat like many of her colleagues. The Scandinavians had once given her the name "conciliatrix".[1] Fried's obituary notice, which appeared in the *Frankfurter Zeitung* on 28 July 1914, placed special emphasis on this side of her character which sought to bring people together:

> She always acted as if a spiritual Geneva convention had already come into existence. But this trait of hers was also the source of her strength as a propagandist. Her refined dignity, which she never permitted to degenerate into passion, was irresistible, and one could not help but be influenced by her. How often we have seen this happen in the course of our congresses! Whenever a clash of opinions arose and there seemed no possibility of agreement being reached, Bertha von Suttner would rise to her feet; and this very act of getting up, her dignified appearance and earnestness of expression caused a calm to come over the gathering which provided a basis for agreement. Her words were received with open hearts.

Material available in the archives shows that as early as 1891, at the Rome congress, she had been active as a "conciliatrix". Differences of opinion had come out into the open as a result of a clash between the representatives of the French peace societies and those of Germany and Austria. The cause of the dispute was the personality of the chairman, Professor Ruggero Bonghi. Shortly before the congress, Bonghi had taken the side of the French in the Alsace-Lorraine issue. The congress was on the brink of collapse. At Bertha Suttner's suggestion, the problem of Alsace-Lorraine was excluded from the agenda, and the congress was able to go ahead.

The national tensions which existed between and sometimes within the individual states of Europe were also reflected in the groups which composed the international peace movement. Bertha Suttner regarded the reduction and, where possible, the elimination of such tensions as one of the crucial tasks of the congresses and also as a necessary precondition for fruitful common endeavour among the individual national societies. In the final session of the 1891 Rome congress she underlined her attitude in no uncertain terms. In her view, politics—by which she also meant party politics and national conflict—should not be a matter for discussion at the congresses.

> From the outset of this congress we have declared in the name of those whom we represent that we have no intention of

playing at politics. We have kept this promise, and our name is to be found against none of the resolutions that concern such matters.[2]

In a document relating to the foundation of the Austrian Peace Society, dated 8 October 1891, stress is laid on the point that the "society will in no way be political". It continues:

There is no need for anyone who becomes a member of the peace movement to swear allegiance to any political creed, and indeed party politics will be specifically excluded from discussion in the Society's meetings.[3]

Again and again she expressed her disapproval of mixing political discussions of the day, party programmes and issues with the work of the peace movement. She put this across both to her fellow campaigners, as in the letter to Ducommun, the Bern Bureau director, which has already been quoted, and to politicians and revolutionaries, as in another letter already quoted, that to W. Liebknecht, which was published in *Vorwärts* and where she stated: "According to principle and statute the members of the peace societies do not as such belong to any party."[4] When she took part on 28 May 1912 in the Paris opening of the "Carnegie Conseil" before she left for the United States, she noted afterwards in her diary: "It is a terrible pity that national issues intrude into our activities."[5]

From the outset of her official role as lady president of the Austrian Peace Society, she had recognised that any deviation from a "purely humanitarian" line into the direction of "political involvement" would on the one hand seriously impede the maintenance of cordial relations between the individual national groups and on the other hand pose a threat to the unity of the movement, put its ideals beyond reach and undermine the credibility of its principles. The present position of the peace movement owes much to her clearheaded assessment of the situation, and the clarity of mind with which she foresaw the possibility that the movement might go into the wrong direction.

She always sought to bring about harmony and reconciliation; and in recognition of this fact she undertook a task at the 1892 Bern congress which debated and accepted a resolution entitled "A European Federation", and signed by E. T. Moneta, the representative of the Italian pacifists, and also by Bertha Suttner. The text ran as follows:

In consideration of the fact that the damage caused by the

armed peace and the constant threat of a great war throughout
the whole of Europe are fundamentally ascribable to the con-
frontation between the various European states without any
framework of law;

in consideration of the fact that a European federation of
states, which would also be in the commercial interests of all
countries, would be in a position to remove this absence of
legality and establish an enduring legal pattern for Europe;

in consideration finally of the fact that such a federation of
states would in no way prejudice the independence of the individual nations as far as their internal affairs are concerned, and
would therefore in no way prejudice their forms of government;

the congress invites the European peace societies and their
supporters to work towards a federation of states on the basis of
their common interests and to make this the highest goal of their
propaganda. It further invites all societies throughout the world
at the time of political elections to point to the necessity for a
standing congress of the nations, which would have placed before
it all international questions, so that every matter of dispute
might be settled on the basis of law, not of force.[6]

The realisation of a "European federation of states" became
one of the primary objectives of the international peace movement. Members of the European societies joined those from the
United States in trying to seek a means of translating the Utopia
of generations gone by into a nineteenth-century reality.

At that time one man in particular was concerned with the
resolution of the economic problems of a European federation,
Sir Max Wächter, and he had proposed a customs union as a
possible basis for economic unification and had personally put
this plan before the heads of the majority of European states.

It was believed that it would be possible to achieve a political
European federation on the model of the United States of
America, or—and this proposal was held by most people to be
the more realistic and practicable—of Pan-America (now the
Organisation of American States), the organisation which brings
together all the states of the American continent. In 1910 Fried
had published a book on the development, structure and significance of the Pan-American movement. In the foreword he expounds an attitude towards a political unification of Europe
which is very much in line with that of the peace movement as a
whole :

When the idea really catches on of setting up an organisation of
European states alongside the American organisation then, I

believe, the path will finally have been found towards peace among the nations of the European world which have suffered so greatly under a weighty burden of hatred and suspicion. Perhaps Europe has already lost its leading position in the world, but it has not yet missed the opportunity of uniting itself.[7]

The seemingly insuperable obstacle confronting those who aspired to see the idea of a federation of European states realised was the enmity between the nations. This problem had to be overcome, and so too had that of stabilising European boundaries. But it seemed that there was a way out of this too. At the fourteenth world peace congress in Lucerne in 1905 a resolution was accepted which recognised that "only the free choice of the inhabitants of a particular territory can determine the national allegiance of that territory" and that, "as soon as this pattern is firmly established, much of the heat will be taken out of the question of coexistence among the nations".[8]

There was an initiative which sought to pave the way towards an accommodation among the warring nations, although not a very successful one : it took the shape of the formation of two-nation committees, for example, between Germany and France, Germany and England, and Austria and Italy. The last of these committees was instituted at the London congress of 1908 by A. H. Fried, Bertha Suttner and E. T. Moneta, and this act was reported to the Austrian Foreign Minister, Baron Ährenthal, in a despatch. The telegram received a polite reply from Vienna, but was sent off only as a private telegram, and did not find its way into the official files. It was a gesture of courtesy on the part of the minister towards Baroness Suttner, but nothing more.

It was the task of this committee, as defined by Bertha Suttner in an article in the *Neue Freie Presse*,

> to employ all possible means to avert the catastrophe of a break between the two countries, and to effect a rapprochement between them; secondly, to work towards a better mutual understanding between the two nations and thus overcome prejudices and sources of enmity which date right back to the days when Austria was regarded by the Italian as the prototype of the oppressive police state and we regarded the Italian as the prototype of low cunning.[9]

But not long after she was recording unhappily in her diary : "Our committee is no more. Austria is suffering from a national malaise. . . ."[10] On 15 January 1909 she discussed the Italian plans with Fried, but a few days later she was taking the view that the Austro-Italian affair "is not within our capabilities". This committee had no success, and when in 1911 Italy went to war against Turkey in Tripoli, the Italian pacifist cause suffered a severe setback. Their friends abroad were deeply hurt not just by the war, but by the approval it met with among many of the leading Italian pacifists. "The damage caused to pacifism by Italy's retrograde step wounds me greatly."[11] The Tripoli war was, in Bertha Suttner's eyes, a terrible warning. She feared that the method the Italians had adopted of declaring war was a fore-taste of things to come, and indeed it was a forerunner of the Blitzkrieg. In speeches which she gave in Budapest on 6 November 1911 and three days later in Bucharest, she expressed her fears openly :

> What an example to set! What a precedent, opening the way for the exercise of force in the future! All the statutes, treaties, obligations, all the basic principles laid down at The Hague have been forgotten, denied as if they had never existed. . . . The action at Tripoli was more than aggression against Turkey, it was an assault on The Hague.[12]

The reports and protocols of the congresses also reveal that on practically every occasion she took the opportunity to speak. She was never content to rest on her laurels, but continued to work towards establishing more and more new contacts and winning over other countries and other continents to the ideas of the peace movement. In this spirit she directed her words at the 1897 Hamburg congress to the peoples of the Far East : "We approach the peoples of Asia, whatever their race, nationality, religion or outlook, with this question : Are they prepared to work together with us in brotherly collaboration for the spread of peace throughout the entire world?"[13] By taking such a step, that is, recognising the equality of the people of those lands which we would nowadays call the developing countries, she was way ahead of the views of many contemporary politicians, who were still thinking in terms of nineteenth-century colonialism.

In the 1904 congress in Boston, she addressed her words specifically to the women present and spoke to them about the "responsibilities and duties of women in the cause."[14] So her activities as "conciliatrix" spread as far as conducting a membership campaign for the peace movement among members of the innumerable women's associations in the United States.

Her activities as a mediator also embraced action on a smaller, more personal scale. The founder of Zionism, Theodor Herzl, asked her to approach the Czar on his behalf to grant him an audience. Herzl, who was horrified at the terrible pogrom in Kishinev in 1903 wanted to tell the Czar in his own words about his idea of a Jewish national state and to ask for assistance for his fellow-believers. The Suttner-Fried collection in the United Nations archives in Geneva contains a draft of a document towards this end in Bertha Suttner's own hand.

These efforts towards reconciliation and negotiation also explain her willingness to take up the cause of Stephanie of Belgium, the widow of Crown Prince Rudolf. Bertha Suttner had met her in Monaco, was invited to their Hungarian estate, and asked by the princess's second husband, Count Lonyay, to publish an article on life in the castle of Oroszvar. "The intention is to let the world know about the domestic happiness and splendour here."[15] At first taken aback by this request, she did in fact write the article, not just out of gratitude to her hosts or to bolster her self-esteem, but out of fellow feeling for the somewhat difficult position of Stephanie at the imperial court in Vienna and in Austrian public life.

Bertha Suttner's attitude of purposeful endeavour, of seeking to help and to reconcile, either by public appeal or by letter or again through the medium of the published word, demands universal admiration. It did not matter to her whether she was seeking to help a princess or the founder of Zionism, whether she was campaigning for members of the peace movement at home or abroad, in Europe or overseas. Her deepest convictions and her love for her neighbour led her to be a "conciliatrix" in the fullest sense of the word.

NOTES

1. *Tagebuch*, 28 April 1906.
2. *Troisième Congrès international de la Paix*, Rome, 1891, p. 162.
3. Library of the United Nations, Geneva, Peace archives, Collection Suttner-Fried (Oo II/79b).
4. *Vorwärts*, Berlin, 20 August 1892.
5. *Tagebuch*, 28 May 1912.
6. *Memoiren*, p. 265.
7. A. H. Fried, *Pan-Amerika, Entwicklung, Umfang und Bedeutung der panamerikanischen Bewegung (1810–1910)*, Berlin, 1910, p. ivf.
8. A. H. Fried, *Handbuch der Friedensbewegung II. Teil*, Berlin & Leipzig, 1913, p. 163.
9. *Neue Freie Presse*, 28 August 1908.
10. *Tagebuch*, 23 November 1908.
11. *Ibid.*, 19 October 1911.
12. *Die Friedens-Warte*, 1911, p. 313.
13. *Bulletin officiel du VIIIe Congrès Universal de la Paix, tenu à Hamburg*, Bern 1897, p. 49.
14. *Official Report of the thirteenth Universal Peace Congress*, Boston, 1904, p. 128.
15. *Tagebuch*, 25 December 1906.

PEACE PROPAGANDA IN THE GRAND MANNER

Referring to Bertha Suttner's organisational talents, Frédéric Passy had dubbed her "notre général en chef". In recognition of her diplomatic gifts, her Scandinavian friends had nicknamed her "conciliatrix". And her international fame continued to be spread with ever new translations of *Lay down your Arms* which came out in European and non-European languages alike.

But any account which confined itself to her achievements among the ranks of the peace movement and her successful literary works, whose primary aim was to spread the ideas of the movement, would offer only a partial picture of her total accomplishments on behalf of the "cause" to which she dedicated so much of her life. Any assessment of this extraordinary woman must inevitably include her attainments in the field of propaganda work on behalf of the peace movement, her public relations activity in the most modern sense of the term and her employment of the most up-to-date means to this end.

She recognised the significance of propaganda at an early stage. At her very first congress in Rome she drew attention to the need for a public campaign on behalf of the peace movement: "I maintain that of all the tasks facing this congress the most urgent is that of propaganda."[1] And to Fried she had once expressed her views in these terms: "We live in the age of the advertisement."[2]

What made her achievement so exceptional was the great variety of different means she employed in the execution of this self-imposed task, and also the success that attended her endeavours, thanks to her singleminded pursuit of this idea and the rigour with which she subordinated all else to it. She left her own peculiar stamp on her publicity campaigns, operating in the grand international manner, entirely free from either petty-minded fanaticism or an excess of feminine sentimentality; it was her generous character and decidedly intellectual personality that gave the tone to her campaigns. She had an unerring instinct for the most subtle shades of meaning in her campaigns on a personal level, as her letters reveal, and equally for the broad sweep of a propaganda exercise directed at a mass impact; and her successes were greater than any a professional public relations man could have achieved.

She had the gift of being able to influence and win over people from a whole variety of backgrounds. On the one hand, she campaigned for an understanding of the ideas of pacifism among the European aristocracy, especially the entourage of Albert I, which included relations and friends of many ruling princes, a not unimportant factor in an age of monarchies. On the other hand, she had already become something of a legend in her own lifetime as the authoress of *Lay down your Arms*; she had become an attraction, a name known to millions, a magnet to the masses. And finally, her work as a journalist, as the writer of pamphlets with explicity "sensational" titles—at least they were sensational at the time—like *Barbarity in the Skies*, *Armament and Over-armament*, or through her regular articles on contemporary affairs,[3] influenced an unknown but not inconsiderable number of people, with her tenacious and persistent efforts based on a method of advertising which depends upon repetition of slogans. To judge by the general level of the papers in which her articles appeared, the readership was on the whole intellectual in character.

NOTES

1. *Troisième Congrès international de la Paix,* Rome, 1891, p. 162.
2. *Tagebuch,* 25 June 1912.
3. These came out under the title of "Randglossen zur Zeitgeschichte", and extracts from the collected "Randglossen" are reproduced in the translation section of this book under the title "The Struggle to prevent World War".

UNOFFICIAL DIPLOMACY

Bertha Suttner was an old hand at the game of "unofficial diplomacy", as a friend of hers once put it, and Monaco, its Prince and his guests offered her the very best of opportunities for putting her ideas and views across to that thin upper crust of European and American society known as the "ruling class". After her first visit to Monaco, Bertha Suttner received a personal handwritten letter from Prince Albert I, inviting her to make an extended stay in the castle as his guest. She gladly accepted, because she felt that "it promotes my cause and my own standing to accept such a friendship—and to stay in such a place".[1] Between 1904 and 1906 she paid annual visits to Monaco, but then declined the invitations for some years, not returning to the principality again until 1911. The main reason behind her giving up these visits, which were of such interest for her, was the conviction that she no longer measured up to the expectations made of her. She did not consider herself enough of an attraction any more in fashionable Monaco life; and she was afraid she would be regarded as too "old hat" to be able to have any real impact even in the little Monaco court. And then she felt herself to be too much of a matron. "I have resolved not to make the journey any more . . . and my gaucherie, general appearance and lack of fine feathers will make me even less of an ornament as the years go by, and that will put an end to my working together with Prince Albert in the cause of peace."[2] And she wrote in 1905 : "I shall not come back again next year—but I should still like to be invited."[3] She really was very taken up with her high reputation as one of the most famous ladies of the day and was ever anxious to play a correspondingly important role among the Prince's circle of friends. She carefully noted down the way the Prince, his guests, and even the servants, conducted themselves towards her, bitterly complaining in her diary about real or imagined snubs, and recording with great delight those conversations with illustrious guests which had interested her, and those times when she had received what she considered to be a fair measure of attention. In such conversations it must have been a source of great satisfaction to her that a concern with the problems of the peace movement had become "fashionable" and "up to the minute"—for this was largely the outcome of her own activities as a propagandist; she herself once wrote in terms of "this condemnation of war which is now very much the fashion".[4]

Those who listened to her in conversation were interested parties indeed. Among those whose name she mentions in her diaries are a Hohenzollern prince, and a sister of the Italian Queen, who was in Monaco with her husband, a Battenberg. Conversations with the Princess inspired her to adopt the plan of one day travelling to Rome and discussing and mediating with Queen Elena, as an Austrian and pacifist, on the dangers of tension between Austria and Italy. Prince Battenberg too held discussions with her:

> Knows me and my book and talks about peace as if he were a d'Estournelles. This was (the Russo-Japanese war) must be the last. People no longer have the right to wage war. It is a crime. In parting, he said to me, "Arbitration will be victorious in the end, and you will have played an important role in bringing this about."[5]

And she had this to say about Prince Ferdinand of Bulgaria: "Horrified at the Japanese war. Works all the time for my ideas in Bulgaria."[6] Or again: "The Duke of Schleswig-Holstein tells me he has read *Lay down your Arms* . . . and when I go to Berlin, I am to tell him, and he will place himself entirely at my disposal."[7] The King of Sweden, Oskar II, also held lengthy conversations with her on her favourite topics:

> I am presented. He salutes me and passes on, going round the company. Then he comes up to me with outstretched hand. I am struck by the beauty of his face. . . . He offers me his hand. "In matters of peace I share your views entirely."—"Your Majesty has demonstrated this already."—"Yes, I am pleased that you recognise that. I have lived through heart-breaking times, and I have only been able to endure because I regard peace as something holy."[8]

Bertha Suttner records that she was held in high esteem, and that her endeavours towards the preservation of peace in Europe were acknowledged, but she was also regarded as an aristocrat, and in Monaco especially this gave her the opportunity to have many valuable audiences, as in Sinaia, where she was received by the Queen of Rumania, who was well known as a poetess under the pseudonym Carmen Sylva. "Something would have been lacking in her life if she had not made my acquaintance."[9] During her stay in Scandinavia, on the occasion of her acceptance of the Nobel Peace Prize, she was received in audience by King Haakon of Norway—"our discussions lasted three quarters of an hour"—and by the King of Denmark, who

> supported the peace movement. Praised Roosevelt.... Said the press was responsible for the mood of war. Recognised my "considerable services." Thought I should have spoken in many other Danish cities. At the end, as he was conducting me to the door, he said : "I call upon God to send his richest blessings upon your fine endeavours, and hope you continue your work !" I replied : "In that, men of power can help—you can help me, your Majesty !"—"I shall do whatever lies within my power."[10]

These contacts flattered her self-esteem, but she also hoped that through these conversations, the political importance of which she clearly exaggerated, much would be done towards the preservation of peace.

But her fame spread beyond the shores of Europe. During her stay in the United States in 1904, on the occasion of the world peace congress in Boston, President Theodore Roosevelt received her. She recorded their meeting in these words :

> It was on 17 September that I was accorded the great honour of being received by the President of the United States and was able to converse with him about those matters which are so dear to my heart. Roosevelt appeared to me as a man of open hearted friendliness, fully conscious of the gravity and import of the matters we discussed. A brave soldier's spirit—and more; the adventurous blood of a frontiersman, but a spirit filled with far-sighted social aspirations, and this is what makes him into a pioneer of the new age. For it was he who was the first to set the Hague Tribunal into operation, and he too intends to summon a new Hague conference. "Worldwide peace is coming," he told me, "it is coming without any doubt, step by step." I had mentioned the Anglo-American arbitration treaty which had been near to settlement in 1897 and said that the time seemed ripe for the resumption of negotiations. "It is my intention," replied the President, "to pave the way towards treaties not just with England, but with all countries : with France, Germany—" I interrupted : "Do not forget my native Austria," and he smiled. "And Austria and Italy as well as England. But England must not be the only other party to the treaty, otherwise it will be thought of as an alliance of the English-speaking peoples.

America should come to terms with all civilised countries at one and the same time. And I have another purpose in mind, that is, that these treaties should have broad terms of reference—with far less restrictions than those which have already been concluded in Europe."[11]

In 1912 Bertha Suttner had a meeting with William Taft, Theodore Roosevelt's predecessor, a great advocate of the idea of a court of arbitration, who, like the supporters of the peace movement, saw in these treaties a more secure foundation for peace throughout the world.

So it was not unnatural that this country, whose successive presidents so openly expressed their sympathy for the principles of the peace movement and for the conclusion of arbitration treaties, should be called "the world of the new future", the "land of boundless possibilities or the land of impossibilities overcome". Bertha Suttner expected all manner of positive things to emerge from this "new world", which was not burdened with the deadweight of past misfortune and was therefore in a position to mould and fashion its own continent according to new and better principles. She was not alone in her faith in America. Count Apponyi wrote to her on 11 July 1904 shortly before the inter-parliamentary conference in the USA: "This meeting in America may well turn out to be the most important so far. The spirit that dwells there will surely exercise some influence upon us Europeans—and on our continent, in their different ways, republics and monarchies have to learn common sense."[12]

The internationally known Austrian international jurist Professor Heinrich Lammasch was trying as late as the beginning of 1918 to hold discussions with Mr. Herron, one of President Woodrow Wilson's advisers, in Bern about the political situation in Austria and Europe as a whole, and to discuss the pattern of territorial boundaries after the war, in order to avoid the possibility of mistakes and to clarify points of obscurity.

All those who had sincerely believed that Europe could be saved by the New World must have been severely disappointed by the inconsistency of the American President and the politicians of the United States after the end of the war. It is not difficult to guess what Bertha Suttner's reaction to the war would have been; it would certainly have come as no great surprise to her.

All in all, it seems to me that the great European disaster is well on the way. If so many seeds have been sown, surely the weeds will sprout up soon—and surely so much stockpiled gunpowder will soon explode?[14]

It is interesting to speculate on her reaction to the collapse of the old empire and the coming of the fateful new European order. Would she have been prepared once more—given that she still had enough physical and mental strength left—to trek round from city to city and from one continent to another like a wandering priest, trying to hold Europe back from the brink of the next catastrophe engendered by the ill-fated peace treaties?

NOTES

1. *Tagebuch*, 27 December 1903.
2. *Ibid.*, 5 April 1905.
3. *Ibid.*, 10 April 1905.
4. *Ibid.*, 26 March 1906.
5. *Ibid.*, 18 March 1905.
6. *Ibid.*, 17 March 1905.
7. *Ibid.*, 17 March 1905.
8. *Ibid.*, 26 March 1906.
9. *Ibid.*, 14 November 1911.
10. *Ibid.*, 1 May 1906.
11. "Drei Wochen in America", in *Stimmen und Gestalten*, Leipzig, 1907, p. 170f.
12. Library of the United Nations, Geneva, Peace archives, Collection Suttner-Fried. Letter from Apponyi to B. v. S., 11 July 1904 (Da 3).
13. M. Lammasch and H. Sperl (eds.), *Heinrich Lammasch. Seine Aufzeichnungen, sein Wirken und seine Politik*, Vienna and Leipzig, 1922, p. 96.
14. *Tagebuch*, 1 April 1913.

LECTURE TOURS

Perhaps she might have done, because several times after her husband's death she had taken upon herself the burden of long lecture tours with the object of showing people the way to a lasting peace. It was of course not possible for her to remove the fear of approaching war from the minds of her audience, but she sought to point out possible means of avoiding it. She was aware of the power of the spoken word, and this is why she accepted invitations to speak in public, although she did not have a high opinion of her own capabilities as a speaker: "I am to speak although I can't. But I must. Just in order to live. If that is so necessary."[1] She often spoke several times in a month in Vienna, travelled to the various cities of the monarchy, to Budapest, Prague, Brno, and many more. She was also invited by friends to go to Bucharest. On the occasion of her acceptance of the Nobel Prize she visited Scandinavian cities and told an interested public about the efforts of the peace movement. She spoke in workers' clubs and in aristocratic circles, to small groups and before invited audiences as well as to students and professors, and in halls that accommodated between four and five thousand people. Her own notes and the published texts of her speeches in the *Friedens-Warte*, as well as newspaper comments, all show that she made reference in her speeches to the events of the day, like the Russo-Japanese war, the Boer war, the Italo-Turkish war, and related them to her own principles and views about peace. She spoke fluently, with "the charm of an unforced mode of speaking and the bell-like clarity of diction of the gifted conversationalist,"[2] or in the words of another report "slowly and distinctly, in impressive, sharp and effectively pointed sentences."[3] Those who found less favour spoke of her as "this lady with the hesitant, somewhat limp manner of talking,"[4] who spoke "with an unmistakable trace of her own Austrian dialect."[5] The meetings she addressed were filled to overflowing: "The hall packed like sardines, standing right up to the platform, much applause."[6] Or: "Hundreds were turned away."[7] After she had spoken, she would receive an ovation, and people would still be "cheering out on the street."[8] But it could also happen that the hall would be packed with "German Nationalists" who heckled her. "Must keep well away from political gatherings. German Nationalists packed the hall. Meeting closed. Moment of panic. Great consternation among those who called the meeting. I found the affair intriguing."[9]

Her appearance like the way she spoke was described and criticised in the press. Some saw her more as a "mater dolorosa" than an apostolic figure with the gift of tongues, and she was mocked for the way she "lisped on against war, clad in elegant black, weighed down with gemstones, an intriguing fan in her hand, fine diction and an outstandingly good posture".[10] Perhaps one Berlin critic offered the most objective assessment of her appearance and her effect upon her auditors:

> Anyone who sees this lady for the very first time immediately regrets having employed phrases to describe her which are not entirely respectful, such as "Bertha of Peace" and the like. Her appearance makes such an aristocratic, one might almost say regal, impression that one is immediately conscious of being in the presence of one who is not merely agitating for something or other in order to make a name for herself, but a personality committed body and soul to her campaign, because she has put her whole heart into this struggle on behalf of humanity, in both senses of the word.[11]

These opinions from the press on her public speeches add up to a picture of a woman demanding respect and admiration, but not without a trace of the comic, even ridiculous about her. Bertha Suttner was all too well aware of the fact that those sections of the press who were opposed to her would offer her no quarter, that she would be branded as an hysterical and power-hungry woman. But she also knew that she had many admirers and supporters already and would continue to win over many more. One of her critics once expressed it in terms which are perhaps not so far short of the truth: "What is so attractive about her tactics in battle is her all-conquering optimism casually sweeping aside all the scorn which has been lavished upon the programme of this 'Fury of Peace' and 'Bertha of Peace'."[12] Hers must have been a strong personality indeed to have overcome all the negative aspects of her appearance, all the unpleasantness which derived from the fact that she was the weaker party, a pacifist in a military age, and a woman getting up on to the platform to speak—at a time when the emancipation of women was still one of the mainstays of the satirical papers—and having overcome them, to win over her audience and generate such great enthusiasm. And she must have been an outstanding propagandist, otherwise the big names in the peace movement would not have invited her to undertake two such important lecture tours as she did. The first, which took sixty eight days (from 10 October to 17 December 1905), during which she visited thirty-one cities of the German Reich, was organised by the Hermann Wolff Bureau in Berlin, and not just by the individual peace societies. Its object was to "exercise some impact on circles outside the ranks of those already converted to the cause".[13] The second grand tour took her through the United States of America and lasted six months (from June to December 1912). She visited more than fifty towns and cities, holding more than one meeting in any one place. The *Friedens-Warte* informed its readers in the June issue for 1912 that

> we European pacifists could find no better ambassador to encourage the support and co-operation of the happier and freer portion of the globe than that woman who for more than twenty years has stood in the front line of the struggle for peace and who . . . embodies not a little of the most admirable aspects of the history of our times.[14]

This American tour had been prepared after a great deal of effort and months of correspondence by a Mrs. Andrea Hofer-Proudfoot, who then accompanied Bertha Suttner as her secretary. Mrs. Hofer-Proudfoot was a descendant of the Tirolese popular hero Andreas Hofer (1767–1810); she belonged to a branch of the family which had emigrated to the USA. In America, she was regarded as a champion of social reform and was a friend of the American publisher Edwin Ginn, a man of pacifist sympathies. At first Bertha Suttner was not enthusiastic towards Mrs. Proudfoot and her plan for an American tour : "In the afternoon Ginn's remarkable friend, A. Hofer-Proudfoot; wants to help. I don't like it. But a remarkable insight into the spirit of the American people",[15] she wrote in her diary and called her "a bundle of energy". But when the tour turned out to be a great and even triumphant success, Bertha Suttner was full of unstinting praise for the organisational and managerial talents of the "bundle of energy".

Some months previously the American press had already "handled the Baroness's journey in detailed articles and dispatches,"[16] and the *Friedens-Warte* again reported that the United Press had stated as early as 20 April that "the Baroness has an unshakeable faith in the power and influence of the great community of American womanhood. It is her intention to visit the great army of the federated women of America and to report to them on the state of darkest war-torn Europe."[17] The plans drawn up by Mrs. Proudfoot did not only provide for visits to the individual peace societies, but in particular to women's clubs. As lady chairman of the peace commission, Bertha Suttner had already spoken about her ideas in the context of the confederation of Austrian women's associations, which had been founded by Marianne Hainisch. She had sought to win over women for her cause by means of lectures to gatherings of women both in Austria and in other countries. And now she was to campaign in the United States among American women for the idea of peace and tell them the facts about the dangers of war in Europe. But she addressed other organisations as well; she spoke in universities and colleges, in Commercial Clubs, in congresses and meetings, for example a "labor federation meeting", in churches and at banquets.

The journey began on 24 May 1912 and took her by way of Paris, where she participated in the opening of the "Carnegie Conseil" and thence to London. On 8 June she set sail from Southampton in the liner *New York*. The whole undertaking was supported by a financial grant from Emanuel Nobel and the Carnegie foundation.

In New York Bertha Suttner was greeted and feted by her friends, but she had to leave immediately for Chicago and Los Angeles. There she addressed the local peace society, but when she got to San Francisco she gave her first great address, as guest of the General Federation of Women's Clubs, an association of "millions of purposeful, energetic women campaigning passionately for the good of mankind".[18] She was received with the greatest enthusiasm in San Francisco, as she was everywhere on her tour which was a triumph from the outset. Bertha Suttner records her surprise in her diary : "The papers celebrate my arrival like that of a queen. . . . They are full of pictures and articles."[19]

The few cuttings from American papers preserved in Geneva archives describe Bertha Suttner as

the most remarkable figure in the world's peace movements. She influenced Alfred Nobel to give his peace prize. In England she is called—the woman who moved the Czar—as it was because of her arguments that he sent out his manifesto for a Hague Tribunal. And yet this powerful lady looks just the kindly, sensible hausfrau, with soft, simply done grey hair, plump uncreased face and a motherly smile.[20]

The tour was a long one with many stopping-off places along the way. It is no longer possible to make an accurate assessment of the number of meetings she actually addressed, for in various cities she spoke more than once; in San Francisco, for example, she had to address no less than six gatherings, a women's congress, a women's club which offered her hospitality, another club in a church (over whose door were inscribed the words "Lay down your arms"), the Commonwealth Club (an association of industrialists), and a special dinner of the association for votes for women; and she addressed yet another meeting in the nearby university town of Berkeley.[21] She wrote home about her first stay in Chicago :

> A great congress awaited me in Chicago : 15,000 teachers, men and women, from every state united in a league which bears the title "National Education Association" meet together for discussion and exchange of views. At this congress I myself have had to give two addresses, one at the peace school meeting and the second at the formal final evening in the large auditorium of the Chicago opera house.[22]

All her reports to the *Friedens-Warte* are in the same vein, as are her entries in her diaries. Nearly every day found her addressing clubs and associations and making new friends. One of the climactic points of her journey must have been her stay in Washington which she notes in her diary :

> Spoke to the club of the women of congress. Banquet. The most magnificent spread I have ever seen in my life, cost around 1,500 to 2,000 dollars, plus national anthem. Diplomats. My speech not diplomatic enough. A bit too accusing and a bit too long. Have a sort of hangover after all that undeserved adulation.[23]

The typescript of one speech she gave on this tour still exists in full. It was given in California, that is to say at the beginning of her journey; later on she did not prepare what she had to say in such detail, and, if what she says in her diary is anything to go by, many of her speeches were off the cuff. She varied her theme to suit her audience and probably hardly ever repeated herself. Her mental alertness had in no way been impaired by the physical strain of the train journeys and the constant change of place. The opposite was the case : the stimulation of staying in what was to her a strange country simply increased her enthusiasm for her task and her work-rate generally. The manuscript of her California speech is of particular interest because of the skill she employs in ensuring that what she has to say is suited to her audience, and also because it shows how quickly she mastered the American journalistic form with its predilection for the slogan. After a few introductory sentences she declares forcibly : "Universal Peace is not a question of possibility, but of necessity!" She praises America, but without being excessively adulatory : "Everything in America can start right. With us Europeans we are eternally busy shaking off the horrors of the past. You are full of strength and courage, and daring, while we grow old struggling for truth." Or when she says : "When people speak to me of the future I tell them—'Go to America and look at the future, for there it has already arrived. They are fifty years in advance of us ethically.' " She turns to the women present and seeks their assistance :

> There is but one help and that is an unmuzzled press, a press in the hands of trained independent peace workers who can tell the truth to the enslaved masses, but which today are not permitted by the ruling institution to think but only to shoot and to shoot each other to uphold their master's prestige.[24]

For the most part, Bertha Suttner stayed with her new friends and was also the guest of many influential personalities. One of the invitations she took up was that from the mother of the newspaper magnate Hearst to her Hazienda Porta da Verona near San Francisco. This lady promised to send her son to see her in Chicago, as he would be interested in Bertha Suttner's journalistic plans. Bertha Suttner also names a Kennedy family in Pittsburgh, dealt with the publisher Ginn, sought to interest Pierpont Morgan for the peace movement, which she did not succeed in doing, and had discussions with William Taft, former United States President, and many other personalities.

During this tour Bertha Suttner still managed to find time between public speaking and social duties to write letters, to campaign for Carmen Sylva and the plight of her little kingdom (there was war between Rumania and Bulgaria), by publishing a letter she received from the Queen in a newspaper, to report back to the *Friedens-Warte* and to prepare with Mrs. Proudfoot a new, abridged translation of *Lay down your Arms* for use in schools.

The months Bertha Suttner spent in the United States imposed a considerable strain upon her, but her diary entries are so full of life and so receptive to every new experience that no reader would suspect that she was an old—or even middle-aged —woman. She admired the social advances of America, was much amused by the very first football match she had seen in her life, and wrote: "Columbia, football game, Missouri lost 29 to nil. I sat as guest of honour in a box with a white banner draped in front of it."[25] She enjoyed being feted, which happened everywhere she went, she revelled in the triumphant successes that attended her, she was delighted at the large numbers who thronged to hear her and was also more than happy with the fact that she was able to measure up to the mental and physical stress of the tour.

In spite of all the excitement she was homesick for Europe. "I feel as if I were on a different planet. And just between us I'll tell you that in spite of all the greatness and splendour, I long to be back in the sheltered, modest circle of my home. There my roots are, and old trees like me...."[26] She firmly turned down an offer to continue her lectures in the USA into January and February: "I am not staying any longer than December. Whether it is homesickness, or whether it is that I want to die there, I must return to Europe before this year is out."[27]

And so she set sail from New York on 14 December 1912.

America, goodbye. I must not be ungrateful. My American journey has shown me wonderful new horizons, brought me much respect and lightened my old age. And this in addition to a windfall of around 20,000 Kroner. And the chance to avoid terribly unpleasant events at home. But what now? What kind of conditions do I find in that shameful medieval country? But here it was quite different. This wealth, this splendour, these boundless possibilities and these vast numbers of people living here to the highest ideals. The young people follow this lead. But of course many bad examples have also been brought here from Europe.[28]

A personal letter from Carnegie told her of another most welcome gift. From 1 January 1913 she was to receive from the Carnegie foundation a monthly pension which guaranteed her a worry-free old age. She never mentions the exact figure in her diaries, but once she said the sum was equivalent to the interest on a capital investment of 100,000 Kroner.

The *Neue Freie Presse* carried the following report on an interview with Mrs. Proudfoot:

Baroness Suttner's journey can without exaggeration be described as of the utmost significance. We travelled no less than 25,000 miles, and more than 400,000 people of all classes declared their readiness to devote their energies to the cause of peace, as did the Federation of Clubs with their million members and the chambers of commerce in every city which passed resolutions on general disarmament and courts of arbitration. In every city we visited we came into contact with the leading citizens, with governors, mayors, senators, high court judges, university chancellors and the like. We were received by President Taft, Bryan, Pierpont Morgan, Andrew Carnegie and many other important people. At all official occasions the Austrian flag was to be seen alongside the stars and stripes in honour of the Austrian guest. It is to be hoped that this great natural advertisement for Austro-Hungary in America will also be reflected in the tourist statistics.[29]

NOTES

1. *Tagebuch,* 8 September 1905.
2. *Neue Hamburger Zeitung,* 4 November 1905.
3. *Breslauer Zeitung,* 2 November 1905.
4. *Leipziger Neueste Nachrichten,* 12 November 1905.
5. *Stettiner Neueste Nachrichten,* 14 November 1905.
6. *Tagebuch,* 11 June 1904.
7. *Ibid.,* 4 December 1904.
8. *Ibid.,* 13 December 1904.
9. *Ibid.,* 27 November 1903.
10. *Der Reichsbote,* Berlin, 15 November 1905
11. *Berliner Tageblatt,* 13 November 1905.
12. *Neue Hamburger Zeitung,* 4 November 1905.
13. *Friedens-Warte,* 1905, p. 183.
14. *Ibid.,* 1912, p. 223.
15. *Tagebuch,* 22 February 1911.
16. *Friedens-Warte,* 1912, p. 222.
17. *Ibid.,* 1912, p. 222.
18. *Ibid.,* 1912, p. 265.
19. *Tagebuch,* 27 & 28 June 1912.
20. *New York Eve World,* 18 June 1912.
21. *Friedens-Warte,* 1912, p. 338.
22. *Ibid.,* 1912, p. 340.
23. *Tagebuch,* 6 December 1912.
24. Library of the United Nations, Geneva, Peace archives, Collection Suttner-Fried (Xye II 8). The full text of her speech is reproduced in the translation section of this book.
25. *Tagebuch,* 19 October 1912.
26. Library of the United Nations, Geneva, Peace archives, Collection Suttner-Fried. B. v. S. to A. H. Fried, letter of 13 July 1912.
27. *Tagebuch,* 3 July 1912.
28. *Ibid.,* 14 December 1912.
29. *Neue Freie Presse,* 29 December 1912.

PROPAGANDA AND JOURNALISM

Bertha Suttner's lecture tour through the United States was an outstanding success from every point of view. It greatly enhanced her prestige and also offered her increased financial security in the shape of the Carnegie foundation pension, which gave her the prospect of a worry-free old age. In addition, she had won vast numbers of new supporters for the peace movement. But despite this, she had failed to realise one of her greatest ambitions: she had hoped to gain the support of one of the big millionaires for the foundation of a pacifist daily newspaper. Since the outset of her work for the peace movement she had repeatedly stressed the importance of an intensive level of propaganda, and towards the end of her American journey she was able to state, on the basis of her experience, that "the idea does not work of its own accord, but through agitation and through 'friends' ".[1] She regarded the newspaper as one of the most effective means of influencing the masses, and this is why she persistently advanced the view that the pacifist movement needed a daily paper of its own. She tried without success to win Emanuel Nobel over to this idea in Marienbad in 1904, and equally Pierpont Morgan "turned her down flat", when she put the proposal before him in New York in 1912.

On the basis of this conviction that the idea must be given practical support in the form of propaganda and active campaigns, she had written two pamphlets in the years 1909 and 1912 respectively, entitled *Armament and Over-Armament* and *Barbarity in the Skies*. The first of these examines the underlying causes of the armaments race, seeks to take the notion ad absurdum, and demonstrates that it is possible to call a halt to the race. The solution would be the unification of Europe, and she concludes her arguments with these words:

> Prophecy is a fool's game. Yet I do not believe that it will be possible to bring about a change in the armaments question by opposing the military, but by enlisting their aid. The transformation of the national armies which stand threatening one another into a reduced policing and defensive force for a united Europe

will have to be carried out by the agreement and collaboration of military circles.[2]

Her *Barbarity in the Skies* is a shattering attempt to warn mankind against the use of the aeroplane, man's ingenious invention, as a weapon of war, and to seek its prohibition in war. Like Cassandra, she foresees death and destruction, and concludes her argument with this appeal :

> In view of the ruinous costs, the dangers threatening our civilisation and the terrors which a spread of war into the newly-conquered skies will hold for any civilised man, we protest against the propaganda which is now all too much in evidence in favour of armed flotillas in the air, and we protest particularly against the practice of dropping bombs from aeroplanes which might fall upon places like hospitals; and we earnestly request those who conduct the affairs of men to arrive with the utmost despatch— if possible before the next Hague conference—at an agreement among the powers with the object of renewing the five-year ban against dropping explosive materials from the air which was introduced at the first Hague conference. In the name of reason and humanity, in the name of the spirit of mankind, whose latest proud achievement paves the way for a period of higher civilisation, in the name of God, which for believer and non-believer alike stands for all that is most noble and elevated which he respects—in the name of all these, may this demand be respected.[3]

The journalistic work which gave her the greatest pleasure, because it corresponded most closely to her personality, that is, it contained polemics, critiques and warnings, was the "Footnotes on contemporary Affairs," which she published every month from 1892 to 1914, with only a short break in the years 1901–1905, first in her journal *Die Waffen nieder!* and then in the *Friedens-Warte*. After her death, Fried edited these commentaries for the publisher Orell Füssli in Zurich.[4] In this two-volume collection her commentaries can be seen to hold up a critical mirror to an age whose rulers feared a catastrophe which would bring universal destruction yet were helping to pave the way towards it through their fateful policies. No study of the period would be complete if it disregarded Bertha Suttner's commentaries. And today her political acumen, her political and historical sense are gaining ever greater recognition, and it is a measure of the great tragedy of her life that her warnings were not understood at the time.

9—SFP * *

The commentaries first appeared in 1892; they discuss problems of the build-up of fleets as well as the various wars, the troubles in the Balkans, votes for women, and much more besides. Once she had recognised the justice of her principles, she stood by them : she took her stand on each of the issues of the day as a convinced pacifist and a human being—but also as an impulsive and high-spirited woman. She is never aggressive, never personally insulting; everything she says bears the stamp of an elegant individual who has the advantage of being able to take a detached view of events. She strikes straight at the heart of the matter, unmasks the hollow pathos and schemings of the press and seeks out the truth. She often appends a warning to her critique, often a plea for the preservation in the future of peace and unity, in an attempt to ward off the great European disaster, the feared and fearful catastrophe.

She did not find the choice of theme a problem :

> There is so much happening, so very much happening in our age, and one learns about things so quickly and in such detail that it would be well-nigh impossible to master and to present within the compass of a brief essay a survey of all the events of an entire month. But since all I have to do is to write about things seen through the eyes of peace, the task is somewhat lightened, for one can ... limit oneself to a consideration of those things which have to do with war and peace, with the constant search to secure peace and parallel threats of war.[5]

Thus she follows all the crises in the development of the sickness of Europe and constantly asserts that unity is the only hope for the continent. About the 1898 Cuba crisis she wrote :

> The insane war (between Spain and the USA), which is being enacted in the new world, should act as a spur to all those who abhor war to work energetically for the establishment of a federation of states in time to prevent the outbreak of war on the European continent.[6]

Or on the occasion of a planned demonstration of naval forces off the Montenegro coast :

> What this means above all else is the coming of "Europe" as a political concept. As the concept of a unity which causes its will to prevail on the apportionment of territory, regulating frontiers, termination of hostilities and the conditions of peace. And not by mere diplomatic notes any more, but through their fleets united in a common demonstration. And as the notion of "Europe"

gains political currency in the daily press, so does the new term "European peace-keeping force". Both are brand new phenomena in real life, but both are demands that pacifists have been making for a very long time.[7]

China appears on the arena of world-wide politics: "China has opened her parliament. One wonders what kind of era is beginning in a land which has for all of us been the epitome of a thousand years of supposed stagnation. As if stagnation has ever existed anywhere."[8]

As an Austrian she naturally took an interest in the internal politics of the monarchy, and one of its principal problems, the measures taken to overcome the conflict between languages. Here too she believed a way out could be found in the establishment of a federation, such as the heir to the throne Franz Ferdinand, then Kaiser Karl I was still aspiring towards carrying through on the advice of Professor Heinrich Lammasch—but the advice came much too late unfortunately.

> The events in the Austrian parliament—sorting out the language problem, obstruction, adjournment—merit relation and discussion at length. But in these pages, which are concerned solely with relationships under international law, must leave such internal political matters to one side. But the connections between internal and external politics spring to mind. The same methods—force, conflict, oppression, chauvinism, the threat of force, opposition in the name of language, culture, individual character—result in a state of war between one nation and another. And the same means of resolving the problem and overcoming the conflict offers itself in both instances: namely, federation.[9]

She wrote with great enthusiasm about a conference of the Empire in London, where the governors of the dominions and commonwealth countries of Canada, Australia, etc., which took place in June 1911, discussed the future of the British Empire: "What is presenting itself there is a federation of free nations, who retain complete sovereignty, with the exception that war between them becomes impossible—a federation open to all, including non-British nations."[10]

She regards the appearance of the first woman in a European parliament as an event of outstanding significance.

> For the first time a woman has entered a European parliament as a deputy. Frl. Rogstad, a teacher, has been elected as a member of the Storting in Christiana. An extremely important event for the women's movement. In her maiden speech on 22 March,

Frl. Rogstad declared that she was a friend of peace, a supporter of arbitration, and expressed the hope that as the rule of force had to give way to the rule of law and justice, wars and militarism will also be done away with one day. None the less she would not vote against a reasonable military budget for the purposes of self-defence. It is fascinating to record that the first woman to act as a parliamentarian speaks on behalf of a future system of international justice with her very first words.[11]

Bertha Suttner was a supporter of the Olympic games:

The reintroduction of the Olympic games by the athletic congress in Paris (from 17 to 23 June), this splendid international gathering presided over by Baron de Courcel, the same man who belonged to the arbitration court which sat on the Behring issue, is an event which could turn out to be one of the most important stages on the path towards the abolition of war. The promotion of physical strength, health and beauty, praised as so beneficial, which is nowadays being employed in military drills, can also be used on another field, and besides the testing of strength on the peaceful ground of the sports arena, carried out by representatives of all nations, a further guarantee of reconciliation. The links between universities should bring together the young people of the various nations on an intellectual level, and the athletic league is a complementary organisation on the plane of physical strength.[12]

But she was also capable of virtuoso writing, as the following extract shows, and it is not difficult to recognise her target even if it is not named in so many words:

I, me, myself! Myself happy and glorious . . . über alles in der Welt! That shall be my motto from now on. I'll have it set to music and sung out loudly and enthusiastically on solemn occasions with glasses raised or during balcony appearances. But perhaps one might also say: What an egoistical, arrogant person that is! That is, instead of "I" it should be "we". And then this "we" becomes like a whole country, for example, the Princedom of Liechtenstein or Lippe-Detmold, and that would be quite thrilling. Lippe-Detmold über alles! Law, life, family, possession, duty, compassion—all these things come afterwards; I—no, we— no, Lippe-Detmold or perhaps some bigger geographical entity über alles. The other I's and the other geographical units may all utter the same cry. What a pretty consort of voices for the community of man.[13]

That is surely a prophetic vision of the thirties of this century, an anticipation of the European tragedy in those years.

Bertha Suttner worked on tirelessly, wrote without let-up, to warn her contemporaries against the threatening danger of world war, to make them aware of the rapidly approaching catastrophe and to arouse their powers of resistance. Even at the age of seventy, when she was tired and beginning to weaken because she was suffering from cancer of the stomach, she worked on at her journalistic schemes and projects, wrote numerous letters and in 1913 went to Prague, Dresden, Berlin, Breslau, Kaiserslauten, to The Hague for the opening of the Peace palace as well as to Paris, and worked with Fried on the plans for the peace congress which was to be held in Vienna in 1914.

In May 1914 she felt her strength draining perceptibly and on the advice of friends went to Styria in Austria to recuperate, and to see her villa which she had purchased a few months previously. She returned to Vienna grievously ill. Her diary entries continued until 2 June. She could see from the tears of her loyal Kathi, who had looked after her for twenty years, and from the shocked faces of her friends, that the end was not far off. Fried remained with her until the last, and it is he who said that her last words were : "Lay down your arms! Tell that to many—many people!"

Her friends and relatives complied with the request she expressed in her will to be cremated in Gotha like her husband, and the urn found its resting place far from Vienna in Gotha. Seven days after her death, on 28 June 1914, those fateful shots were fired in Sarajevo and the European catastrophe took its course.

NOTES

1. *Tagebuch*, 28 November 1912.
2. *Rüstung und Überrüstung*, Berlin, 1909, p. 70.
3. *Die Barbarisierung der Luft*, Berlin, 1912, p. 31f.
4. *Der Kampf um die Vermeidung des Weltkrieges. Randglossen aus zwei Jahrzehnten zu den Zeitereignissen vor der Katastrophe*, Zurich, 1917. Extracts from this work are reproduced in the translation section of this book.
5. *Der Kampf um die Vermeidung des Weltkrieges*, Zürich, 1917, vol. i, p. 3. Article for September 1892. (Subsequent notes to this chapter give volume and page number, followed by the date the actual article was written in brackets.)
6. i, 479 (April 1898).
7. ii, 475 (April 1913).
8. ii, 479 (April 1913).
9. ii, 399 (June 1897).
10. ii, 349 (September 1911).
11. ii, 318 (April 1911).
12. i, 140 (July 1894).
13. ii, 11 (February 1907).

POSTSCRIPT

Did Bertha Suttner live, work, fight and suffer in vain? It is so tempting to answer to this question in the affirmative, in view of the catastrophies of recent decades which seem to vindicate those who maintain that people will never change, that things will always be like this and that there will always be wars.

But on the other side of the coin, the League of Nations was set up after the First World War and sought to preserve the peace, the Kellog-Pact outlawed war, and after the Second World War came the United Nations which has continued to strive until the present day to resolve international conflict by peaceful means. In Strasbourg the Council of Europe has been established, and the European Economic Community has been working towards economic unity in Europe. An international peace-keeping force was raised by the UNO General Secretary of the day, Dag Hammarskjöld. This list of achievements could be considerably extended—but could they not all be traced back to the early pioneering days, to the "castles in the air" of a group of idealists in the nineteenth century, most of whom were in touch with Bertha Suttner, if they were not her actual comrades-in-peace? It is an unbroken chain; the word is passed on from one generation to the next.

Seen from this standpoint, the first steps of the peace movement, which have often been scorned and grossly underrated, assume new weight and significance. In looking back at the nineteenth century, it becomes clear how much of an age of new beginnings it was, an age which paved the way to great upheavals and catastrophes—but also to positive and constructive change.

Bertha Suttner stood in the front line of this hard-fought battle for humanity and world peace, knowing full well that she would be misunderstood, that people would refuse to credit her, that she would be laughed to scorn, and that she personally would never come within sight of her goal. And yet she fought on with the only weapons she knew, the spoken and written word, fought on against the tide of history. This she did with invincible optimism, with a sense of duty hardly less strong than that of the military man, and with the conviction that even a solitary voice should and must point out the right path, that she would ultimately succeed if she persistently proclaimed her beliefs to her fellow men with all the sincerity she could muster.

Even though all the objectives that Bertha Suttner had set herself have not been attained even today, what has none the less been achieved, despite many setbacks, more than justifies the optimism of this extraordinary woman. Her conduct, her brave life and tireless endeavour were to be an example to generations to come, giving them the courage not to lose faith in their fellow men but to look with confidence to the future.

THE WRITINGS OF
BERTHA VON SUTTNER

HOW I CAME TO WRITE
"LAY DOWN YOUR ARMS"

It was the end of the eighties. I had already reached mature years and was studying scientific, philosophical and historical works with the greatest zeal, when the realisation slowly began to dawn on me which soon became an unshakeable conviction, that war was an institution handed down to us from the dark ages of the past which civilisation had to eliminate. At the same time I found out that there was a society in England based on such views and working towards the introduction of international arbitration by influencing public opinion.

I lost no time in writing to this society, the Peace and Arbitration Association, as it was called, to obtain the necessary information. Hodgson Pratt, who died only recently at an advanced age, was the founder and chairman of the organisation and sent me by return the rules and publications of the society. Ever since that time we had been in correspondence. And that is how I got to know about all the things that had been achieved in this important field and what still remained to be done.

The more I learned about the subject, the greater the fascination it exercised on me, and the more eager I became to do all that lay within my feeble powers to advance the cause of the peace movement. Since I had devoted myself to the profession of letters, it seemed clear to me that the most appropriate area for me to work in was literature. I had originally decided to write a little story about a young woman who loses her husband, whom she loves deeply, on the battlefield and as a result came round to condemning war, as gradually as I myself had. Of course, in my own case my convictions are founded entirely upon theory, whereas my heroine was to arrive at this view on the basis of her own actual experiences.

As I was busying myself with gathering the necessary material for my little story, the subject began to take on such substantial proportions and became such a preoccupation for me that, instead of the novelette I had planned, a two-volume novel came into being. I was no longer content with superficial bits and pieces of information but embarked upon the study of recognised authorities on the subject, and read through reports on the campaigns of 1859, 1864, 1866, and 1870–71, and the memoirs of various generals, examined the records of surgeons, military doctors and the Red Cross Society, rummaged through libraries and archives, and also looked over the diplomatic despatches which were exchanged during those periods among the armies involved.

Armed with such source material, I was able to set about constructing my book on a firm historical foundation, and to develop a plot whose central theme was a strong campaign against war. And when I had written the word "Finis" on the last page of the manuscript and the title *Lay down your Arms* on the first, I felt that I was now really in a position to achieve something for a cause which was so dear to my heart. I was armed for the battle!

I confidently despatched my book to a Suttgart editor who had hitherto accepted everything else I sent him, and had only a short time before asked me if I would let him have something new. But the manuscript was returned to me in all haste with the comment: "We very much regret that we are unable to accept this novel." So I tried other editors, but they all turned me down with reasons like "The subject would not be of interest to our readers", or "It would offend many of our readership", or again "It is quite impossible to publish anything of this nature in a modern military state". Such were the views of the leading journals in Germany at that time.

So I turned my attention to the book publishers and first of all sent my manuscript to my publisher Pierson in Dresden. He kept it for a long time; finally he advised me to change the title, which he called too aggressive, and to send the manuscript to some authoritative person who would study it carefully with a view to expunging or modifying those passages which in political or military circles might give offence. I resolutely refused to have anything to do with this proposal. The title of the book expressed precisely the thought which had been at the centre of my mind all through the process of writing, and so the reader could tell from the outside cover what to expect from the text itself; and the very passages which he had in mind to exclude for fear of offending certain groups of people were those which contained the *raison d'être* of my book. So I would not accept any alterations, neither in the title nor in the body of the text.

When I later became personally involved in the work of the

peace movement, many people believed that I had written my book as a result of my involvement. But the truth was quite the reverse. It was the cause of my involvement.

LAY DOWN YOUR ARMS

My father was a general in the Austrian army, and had fought at Custozza under "Father Radetzky", whom he venerated to superstition. What eternal campaigning stories had I to listen to! Dear Papa was so proud of his warlike experiences, and spoke with such satisfaction of the campaigns in which he had fought, that I felt an involuntary pity for every man who possessed no such reminiscences. But what a drawback for the female sex to be excluded from this most magnificent display of the manly feeling of honour and duty! If anything came to my ears about the efforts of women after equality—and of this in my youth but little was heard, and then usually in a tone of contempt and condemnation—I conceived the wish for emancipation only in one direction, *viz.*, that women also should have the right to carry arms and take the field. Ah, how beautiful was it to read in history about a Semiramis or a Catherine II. "She carried on war with this or that neighbouring state—she conquered this or that country!"

Speaking generally it is history which, as our youth are instructed, is the chief source of the admiration of war. From thence it is stamped on the childish mind that the Lord of armies is constantly decreeing battles, that these are, as it were, the vehicle upon which the destiny of nations is carried on through the ages, that they are the fulfilment of an inevitable law of nature and must always occur from time to time like storms at sea or earthquakes; that terror and woe are indeed connected with them; but the latter is fully counterpoised, for the commonwealth by the importance of the results, for individuals by the blaze of glory which may be won in them, or even by the consciousness of the fulfilment of the most elevated duty. Can there be a more glorious death than that on the field of honour, a nobler immortality than that of the hero? All this comes out clear and unanimous in all school-books or "readings for the use of schools," where, besides the formal history, which is only represented as a concatenation of military events, even the separate tales and poems always manage to tell only of heroic deeds of arms. This is a part of the patriotic system of education. Since out of every scholar a defender of his country has to be formed, therefore the enthusiasm even of the child must be aroused for this its first duty as a citizen; his spirit must be hardened against the natural horror which the terrors of war might awaken, by passing over as quickly as possible the story of the most fearful massacres and butcheries as of something quite common and necessary, and laying meanwhile all possible stress on the ideal side of this ancient national custom; and it is in this way they have succeeded in forming a race eager for battle and delighting in war.

The girls—who indeed are not to take the field—are educated out of the same books as are prepared for the military training of the boys, and so in the female youth arises the same conception which exhausts itself in envy that they have nothing to do with war and in admiration for the military class. What pictures of horror out of all the battles on earth, from the Biblical and Macedonian and Punic Wars down to the Thirty Years' War and the wars of Napoleon, were brought before us tender maidens, who in all other things were formed to be gentle and mild; how we saw there cities burnt down and the inhabitants put to the sword and the conquered trodden down—and all this was a real enjoyment; and of course through this heaping up and repetition of the horrors the perception that they were horrors becomes blunted, everything which belongs to the category of war comes no longer to be regarded from the point of view of humanity, and receives a perfectly peculiar mystico-historico-political consecration. War must be—it is the source of the highest dignities and honours—*that* the girls see very well and they have had also to learn by heart the poems and tirades in which war is magnified.

(pp. 3–4)

There had been now for a long time a certain black point visible on the political horizon, about the possible increase of which the liveliest commentaries were made in all journals and at all private parties. I had up to that time thought nothing about it. My husband and my father and their military friends might have often said in my hearing, "There will soon be something to settle with Italy," but it glanced off my understanding. I had little time or inclination to trouble myself about politics.

So that however eagerly people about me might debate about the relations between Sardinia and Austria, or the behaviour of Napoleon III, of whose help Cavour had assured himself by taking part in the Crimean War, or however constantly they might talk about the tension which this alliance had called forth between us and our Italian neighbours, I took no notice of it.

But on April 1 my husband said to me very seriously :—

"Do you know, dear, that it will soon break out?"

"What will break out, darling?"

"The war with Sardinia."

I was terrified. "My God! that would be terrible! And will you have to go?"

"I hope so."

"How can you say such a thing? Hope to leave your wife and child!"

"If duty calls."

"One might reconcile oneself to it; but to hope—which means wish—that such a bitter duty should arise!"

"Bitter! A rattling jolly war like that must be something glorious! You are a soldier's wife; don't forget that."

I fell on his neck. "O my dear husband, be content. I also can be brave! How often have I sympathised with the heroes and heroines of history! What an elevating feeling it must be to go into battle! If I only might fight, fall, or conquer at your side!"

"Bravely spoken, little wife, but nonsense! Your place is here, by the cradle of the little one, who also is to become a defender of his country when he is grown up. Your place is at our household hearth. It is to protect this, and guard it from any hostile attack, to preserve peace for our homes and our wives, that we men have to go to battle."

I don't know why, but these words, which, or something of the same sort, I had often before heard and read with assent, this time seemed to me to be in a sense mere "phrases". There was certainly no hearth menaced, no horde of barbarians at the gate, merely a political tension between two cabinets. So, if my husband was all on fire to rush into the war, it was not so much from the pressing need of defending his wife, child, and country, but much rather his delight in the march out, which promised change and adventure—his seeking for distinction and promotion. "Oh, yes," was my conclusion from this train of thought,

"it is ambition—a noble, honourable ambition—delight in the brave discharge of duty."
(pp. 11–12)

My father, also, was all on fire for the war. To conquer the Piedmontese would be only child's play; and, in support of this assertion, the Radetzky anecdotes were poured out again. I heard the impending campaign talked about always from the strategic point of view—*i.e.*, a balancing of the chances on the two sides; how and where the enemy would be routed, and the advantages which would thereby accrue to "us". The humane point of view, *viz.*, that whether lost or won every battle demands innumerable sacrifices of blood and tears, was quite left out of sight. The interests which were here in question were represented as raised to such a height above any private destiny, that I felt ashamed of the meanness of my way of thinking, if at times the thought occurred to me: "Ah! what joy do the poor slain men, the poor cripples, the poor widows, get out of the victory?" However, very soon the old school-book dithyrambs came in again for an answer to all these despairing questionings: "Glory offers recompense for all". Still—suppose the enemy wins? This question I propounded in the circle of my military friends, but was ignominiously hissed down. The mere mention of the possibility of a shadow of a doubt is in itself unpatriotic. To be certain beforehand of one's invincibility is a part of a soldier's duties; and, therefore, in her degree, of those of a loyal wife of a lieutenant.
(pp. 13–14)

The house bell rang. I dried my eyes at once. Who could it be so early?

It was my father. He rushed in all in a hurry.

"Now, children," he cried, all out of breath, throwing himself into an arm-chair. "Have you heard the great news? The ultimatum ——"

"I have just told my wife."

"Tell me, dear papa, what you think," I asked anxiously. "Will that prevent the war?"

"I am not aware that an ultimatum ever prevented a war. It would indeed be only prudent of this wretched rabble of

Italians to give in and not expose themselves to a second Novara.
Ah! if good Father Radetzky had not died last year I believe
he would, in spite of his ninety years, have put himself again at
the head of his army, and, by God! I would have marched along
with him. We two have, I think, shown already how to manage
these foreign scum. But it seems they have not yet had enough of
it, the puppies! They want a second lesson. All right. Our Lom-
bardo-Venetian kingdom will get a handsome addition in the
Piedmontese territory, and I already look forward to the entry
of our troops into Turin."

"But, papa, you speak just as if the war were already declared,
and you were glad of it! But how if Arno has to go too?" And
the tears were already in my eyes again.

"That he will too—the enviable young fellow!"

"But my terror! The danger ——"

"Eh! what? Danger! 'A man may fight and not be slain,' as
the saying goes. I have gone through more than one campaign,
thank God, and been wounded more than once—and yet I am
all alive, just because it was ordained that I should live through
it."

The old fatalist way of talking! the same as prevailed to settle
Ruru's choice of a profession—and which even now appeared to
me again as quite philosophical.

"Even if it should chance that my regiment is not ordered
out ——" Arno began.

"Ah, yes!" I joyfully broke in, "there is still that hope."

"In that case I would get exchanged, if possible."

"Oh, it will be quite possible," my father assured him. "Hess
is to receive the command-in-chief and he is a good friend of
mine." My heart trembled, and yet I could not help admiring
both the men. With what a joyful equanimity they spoke of a
coming campaign, as if it were only a question of some pleasure
trip that had been arranged. My brave Arno was desirous, even
if his duty did not summon him, to go and meet the foe, and my
magnanimous father thought that quite simple and natural. I
collected myself. Away with childish, womanish fear! Now was
the time to show myself worthy of this my love, to raise my heart
above all egotistic fears and find room for nothing but the noble
reflection—"my husband is a hero".

I sprang up and stretched out both my hands to him: "Arno,
I am so proud of you!"

He put my hands to his lips, then turned to papa and said, with a face radiant with joy : —

"You have brought the girl up well, father-in-law!"

Rejected! The ultimatum rejected! This took place at Turin, April 26. The die is cast! War has broken out.
(pp. 15–17)

For a week I had been prepared for the catastrophe, and yet its occurrence gave me a bitter blow. I threw myself sobbing on the sofa, and hid my face in the cushion when Arno brought me the news.

He sat down by me, and began gently to comfort me.

"My darling! Courage! Compose yourself! It is not so bad after all. In a short time we shall return as conquerors. Then we two shall be doubly happy. Do not weep so—it breaks my heart. I am almost sorry that I have engaged to go in any case. But, no; just think, if my comrades are forced to go, with what right could I remain at home? You yourself would feel ashamed of me. No. I must experience the baptism of fire some time, and till that has happened I do not feel myself truly a man or a soldier. Only think how delightful if I come back with a third star on my collar—perhaps with the cross on my breast."

I rested my head on his shoulder, and kept on weeping the more. But I reflected how small such things were. Stars and crosses seemed to be at that moment only empty spangles. Not ten grand crosses on that dear breast could offer me any recompense for the terrible possibility that a ball might shatter it.

Arno kissed me on the forehead, put me softly aside, and stood up.

"I must go out now, my dear, to my colonel. Have your cry out. When I come back I hope to find you firm and cheerful. That is what I have need of, and not to be shaken with sad anticipations. At such a decisive moment as this my own dear little wife surely will do nothing to take the heart out of me or damp my ardour for exploits? Good-bye, my treasure." And he departed.

I collected myself. His last words were still ringing in my ears. Yes, plainly my duty now was not merely not to damp, but as far as possible to increase, his spirit and his ardour for exploits. That is the only way in which we women can exercise our patriotism, in which we can take any share in the glory our husbands

bring from the battlefields. "Battlefields"—it is surprising how
this word suddenly presented itself to my mind in two radically
different meanings. Partly in the accustomed historical significa-
tion, so pathetic, and so calculated to awake the highest admiration; partly in the loathsomeness of the bloody, brutal syllable
"fight". Yes, those poor men who were being hurried out had
to lie stricken down on the field, with their gaping, bleeding
wounds, and among them perhaps—and a loud shriek escaped
me as the thought passed through my mind.

My maid Betty came running in all in a fright. "For God's
sake, my lady, what has happened?" she asked trembling.

I looked at the girl. Her eyes also were red with weeping.
I guessed; she knew the tidings already, and her lover was a
soldier. I felt as if I could press my sister in misfortune to my
heart.

"It is nothing, my child," I said softly. "Those who go away
will surely return."

"Ah, my gracious lady, not all," she replied, breaking out
anew into tears.

(pp. 19–20)

It was a time of excitement. The war "has broken out". People
forget that it is really two masses of men who are rushing to fight
each other, and conceive of the event as if it was some exalted
overruling third power, whose outbreak compels these two masses
into the fight. The whole responsibility fall on this power, lying
beyond the wills of individuals, and which on its side merely produces the fulfilment of the destined fate of the nations. Such is
the dark and awful conception which the majority of mankind
have of war, and which was mine too. There was no question of
my feeling any revolt against making war in general. What I
suffered from was only that my beloved husband had to go into
the danger and I to stay behind in anxiety and solitude. I rummaged up all my old impressions from the days of my historical
studies, in order to strengthen and inspire me with the conviction
that it was the highest of human duties which called my dear one
away, and that thereby the possibility was offered to him of
covering himself with glory and honour. Now at any rate I was
living in the midst of an epoch of history, and this again was a
peculiarly elevating thought. Since from Herodotus and Tacitus,
down to the historians of modern times, wars have always been

represented as the events of most importance and of weightiest consequence, I concluded that at the present time also a war of this sort would pass with future historians as an event to serve for the title of a chapter.

This elevated tone, overpowering in its impressiveness, was that which prevailed everywhere else. Nothing else was spoken of in rooms or streets, nothing else read in the newspapers, nothing else prayed about in the churches. Wherever one went one found everywhere the same excited faces, the same eager talk about the possibilities of the war. Everything else which engaged the people's interest at other times—the theatre, business, art— was now looked on as perfectly insignificant. It seemed to one as if it were not right to think of anything else whilst the opening scene in this great drama of the destiny of the world was being played out. And the different orders to the army with the well-known phrases of the certainty of victory and promise of glory; and the troops marching out with clanging music and waving banners; and the leading articles and public speeches conceived in the most glowing tone of loyalty and patriotism; the eternal appeal to virtue, honour, duty, courage, self-sacrifice; the assurances made on both sides that their nation was known to be the most invincible, most courageous, most certainly destined to a higher extension of power, the best and the noblest—all this spread around an atmosphere of heroism, which filled the whole population with pride and called out in each individual the belief that he was a great citizen in a great state.

(pp. 22–3)

"Now, Martha, it is all over. Solferino was decisive—we are beaten."

My father came hastily one morning on to the terrace, with these words, where I was sitting under the shadow of a clump of lime trees.

I had gone back home to the house of my girlhood, with my little Ruru. A week after the great battle, which had struck me down, my family moved to Grumitz, our country house in Lower Austria, and I with them. I should have been in despair alone. Now all were again around me, just as before my marriage—papa, Aunt Mary, my little brother, and my two growing sisters. All of them did what they possibly could to mitigate my grief, and treated me with a certain consideration which did me good. Evidently they found in my sad fate a sort of consecration, a something which raised me above those around me, even a kind of merit. Next to the blood which soldiers pour out on the altar of their country, the tears which the bereaved mothers, wives, and sweethearts of the soldiers pour on the same altar become a libation hardly less sacred. And thus it was a slight feeling of pride, a consciousness that to have lost a beloved husband on the field of honour conferred a kind of military merit, which helped me most to bear my pain; and I was far from being the only one. How many, ah! how many women in the whole of the country were then mourning over their loved ones sleeping in Italian earth!

At that time no further particulars were known to me of Arno's end. He had been found dead, recognised, and buried. That was all I knew. His last thought doubtless had flown towards me and our little darling, and his consolation in the last moment must have been : "I have done my duty, and more than my duty".

"We are beaten," repeated my father gloomily, as he sat down by me on the garden seat.

"So those who have been sacrificed were sacrificed in vain." I sighed.

"Those who have been sacrificed are to be envied, for they know nothing of the shame which has befallen us. But we will soon pick up again for all that, even if at present peace, as they say, must be concluded."

"Ah, God grant it," I interrupted. "Too late, indeed, for my poor Arno, but still thousands of others will be spared."

"You are always thinking of yourself and of individuals. But in this matter it is Austria which is in question."

"Well dear, a kingdom, a state, lives a longer and more important life than individuals do. They disappear, generation after generation, while the state expands still farther, grows into glory, greatness and power, or sinks and crumples up and disappears, if it allows itself to be overcome by other kingdoms. Therefore the most important and the highest aim for which any individual has to struggle, and for which he ought to be glad to die, is the existence, the greatness and the well-being of the kingdom."

(pp. 40–1)

I turned to Baron Tilling.

"And what say you? have you heard of Darwin, and do you reckon yourself among his followers or opponents?"

"I have heard a good deal about the matter, countess, but I have formed no judgement on it; for as to the work under discussion, *The Origin of Species*, I have not read it."

"I must confess," said the doctor, "that I have not either."

"*Read* it? Well, to be sure, I have not either," said the Minister.

"Nor I—nor I—nor I," came from the rest.

"But," the Minister proceeded, "the subject has been so much spoken of, the cant words of the system 'fight for existence,' 'natural selection,' 'evolution,' etc., are in everybody's mouth, so that one can form a clear conception of the whole matter and select a side decidedly with its supporters or opponents, to which first class, to be sure, belong only some Hotspurs who love violent changes and are always grasping after effect, while the cool, strictly critical people, who demand proof positive, cannot possibly choose any other than the position of opponents—shared by so many specialists of consideration—a position which, to be sure ——"

"That can hardly be positively asserted," said Tilling, reviewing the whole matter, "unless one knows the position of its supporters. In order to know what the strength of the opposing arguments is, which, as soon as a new idea comes up, are heard shouting in chorus all round it, one must oneself have penetrated into the idea. It is generally the worst and weakest reasons which are repeated by the masses with such unanimity; and on such grounds I do not choose to pass a judgement. When the theory of Copernicus came up, only those who had gone through the labour of following the calculations of Copernicus could see that they were correct: the others, who guided their judgement by the anathemas which were thundered against the new system from Rome ——"

"In our century," interrupted the Minister, "as I observed before, scientific hypotheses, if incorrect, are no longer rejected on the grounds of orthodoxy but of science."

"Not only if incorrect," answered Tilling, "but even when they are going afterwards to be established, new hypotheses are always at first controverted by the old fogeys of science. This set does not like even in our day to be shaken in their long-accustomed views and dogmas—just as at that time it was not only the fathers of the Church but the astronomers also who were zealous in attacking Copernicus."

"Do you mean by this," broke in the rough-speaking general, "that this ape-notion of our eccentric Englishman is as correct as that the earth goes round the sun?"

"I will make no assertion at all about it, because, as I said, I do not know the book. But I will make a point of reading it. Perhaps (but only perhaps, for my knowledge of such matters is only slight) I shall then be able to form a judgement. Up to the present time I must confine myself to supporting my opinion on the fact that this theory meets with widespread and passionate opposition—a fact, 'to be sure,' which, to my mind, speaks rather for than against its truth."

"You brave, straightforward, clear spirit," said I to myself, apostrophising the speaker.

(pp. 68–9)

It was in the morning of 20th June. All the details of this memorable day remain impressed on my memory. Oppressive heat prevailed outside, and to shut this out the Venetian blinds had been let down in my room. Covered with light, loose clothing, I was lying exhausted on the sofa. I had passed an almost sleepless night, and had now shut my eyes in a dreamy half-doze. Near me on my table was standing a vase with some powerfully smelling roses. Through the open window the sound of a distant exercise in trumpet-playing came in. Everything was provocative of slumber, yet consciousness had not quite left me. Only one half of it—I mean that of care—had departed. I had forgotten the danger of war and the danger that stood before myself. I knew only that I was alive—that the roses, along with the rhythm of the *reveillé* which the trumpeter was playing, were giving out sweet soothing influences—that my beloved husband might come in at any minute, and if he saw me asleep would only tread in the lightest manner so as not to awaken me. I was right; next minute the door opposite to me opened. Without raising my lids I could see through a tiny cleft between the eyelashes that it was he whom I was expecting. I made no attempt to rouse myself from my half-slumber, for by doing so I might chase away the whole picture; for it might be that the appearance at the door was only the continuation of a dream, and it might be that I was only dreaming that I had opened my eyelids ever so little. So now I shut them entirely and took pains to continue the dream—that the dear one came closer, that he bent over me and kissed my forehead.

And so indeed it was. Then he knelt down by my couch and remained motionless for a while. The roses were still breathing and the distant horn playing its tra-ra-ra.

"Martha, are you asleep?" I heard him ask softly.

Then I opened my eyes.

"For God's sake, what is it?" I cried out, frightened to death, for the countenance of my husband as he knelt by me was so deeply overclouded by sorrow that I guessed at once that some misfortune had happened. Instead of replying he laid his head on my breast.

I understood all. He had to go. I had thrown my arm round his neck, and we remained both in the same position for some time without speaking.

"When?" I asked at length.

"Early to-morrow morning."

"Oh, my God! my God!"

"Calm yourself, my poor Martha."

"No, no, let me weep. My misfortune is too great, and I know —I see it in your face—so is yours. Never did I see so much pain in any human face as I have just read in your features."

"Yes, my wife. I am unfortunate to have to leave you in such a moment ——"

"Frederick, Frederick; we shall never see each other again. I shall die ——"

"Or I shall fall. Yes, I believe it, too; we shall never see each other again!"

(pp. 143–5)

For several weeks I hovered between life and death. My child died the day of his birth. The mental pain, which parting from my beloved husband had caused me, just at the time when I wanted all my strength to master the bodily pain, had rendered me incapable of bearing up against it, and I was near succumbing altogether.

The physician was obliged by his plighted word to send my poor husband the sorrowful news that the child was dead, and the mother in danger of death.

As to the news which came from him, they could not be com-

municated to me. I knew no one and was delirious day and night.
A strange delirium. I brought back with me a feeble reminiscence
of it into the period of recovered consciousness, but to reproduce
this in reasonable words would be impossible for me. In the ab-
normal whirl of the fevered brain, conceptions and images form
themselves for which there is no expression in language suitable
to our normal thoughts. Only so much can I set down—and I
have attempted to fix the fantastic sketch in the red volumes—
that I confused the two events—the war and my confinement—
together. I fancied that cannon and naked weapons (I distinctly
felt the bayonet thrusts were the instruments of delivery, and
that I was lying there the prize of contention between two
armies rushing on each other. That my husband had marched out
I knew, but I saw him still in the form of the dead Arno, while
by my side Frederick dressed as a sick nurse was stroking the
silver stork. Every moment I was awaiting the bursting shell
which was to shatter us all three—Arno, Frederick, and me—to
pieces, in order that the child could come into the world, who
was destined to rule over "Denstein, Schlesmark, and Holwig."
. . . And all this gave me such unspeakable pain and was so
unnecessary. . . . There must, however, be some one somewhere
who could change it and remove it all, who could lift off this
mountain from my heart and that of all humanity by some
word of power; and I was devoured with a longing to cast myself at this somebody's feet and pray to him : "Help us! for
the sake of mercy and justice help us! Lay down your arms!
down!" With this cry on my lips I woke one day to consciousness. My father and Aunt Mary were standing at the foot of
the bed, and the former said to me to hush me :—

"Yes, yes, child, be quiet. All arms down."

This recovery of the sense of personality after a long sus-
pension of the intellect is certainly a strange thing. First the joyful
astonished discovery that one is alive, and then the anxious
questioning with oneself who one really is . . .

But the sudden answer to that question, which burst in with
full light upon me, changed the just awakened pleasure of existence into violent pain. I was the sick Martha Tilling, whose
newborn child was dead, and whose husband was gone to
battle. . . . How long ago? That I knew not.

"Is he alive?—have you letters there?—messages?" were my
first questions. Yes; there was quite a little heap of letters and
telegrams piled up which had come during my illness. Most of

them were merely inquiries after *my* condition, requests for daily, and as far as possible, hourly information. This, of course, was so long as the writer was at places where the telegraph could reach him.

I was not permitted to read Frederick's letters at once; they thought it would excite me too much and disturb me; and now that I was hardly awake out of my delirium I must, before all things, have repose. They could tell me as much as this: "Frederick was unhurt up to the present time". He had already been through several successful engagements. The war must now soon be over. The enemy maintained themselves at Alsen only; and if this position once were taken our troops would return, crowned with glory. This was what my father said for my comfort, and Aunt Mary gave me the history of my illness. Several weeks had now passed since her arrival, which was the very day on which Frederick departed, and my child was born and died. Of that I had preserved a recollection, but what passed in the interval—my father's arrival—the news that had come from Frederick—the course of my illness—of all that I knew nothing. Now I heard for the first time that my condition had become so much worse that the medical men had quite given me up, and my father had been called to see me "for the last time". The bad news must certainly have been sent to Frederick; but the better news also—for the doctors had given hope again some days ago —must by this time have reached him.

"If he himself is still alive," I struck in, with a deep sigh.

"Do not commit a sin, Martha," my aunt admonished me; "the good God and His saints would not have preserved you, in answer to our prayers, in order afterwards to send such a visitation upon you. . . .

(pp.149–51)

Next day, on my urgent prayer, I was permitted to read through all the messages that had come from Frederick. Mostly they were only questions in a single line, or news equally laconic. "An engagement yesterday. I am unhurt." "We march again to-day. Send messages to ———" A longer letter bore this direction on the envelope: "To be delivered only if all danger is over". This I read last :—

"My all! Will you ever read this? The last news which reached me from your physician ran : 'Patient in high fever; condition

grave'. 'Grave!' He used the expression perhaps out of consideration, so as not to say 'Hopeless'. If you have this put into your
hands you will know by that that you have escaped the danger;
but you may think, in addition, what my feelings were, as, on
the eve of a battle, I pictured to myself that my adored wife was
lying on her deathbed; that she was calling for me, stretching
out her arms for me. We did not even say any regular adieu to
each other; and our child, about whom I had had such joy,
dead! And to-morrow, I myself—suppose a bullet find me? If I
knew beforehand that you were no more, the mortal shot would
be the dearest thing to me; but if you are preserved—no! then I
do not wish to know anything more of death. The 'joy of dying,'
that unnatural feeling which the field preachers are always pressing on us, is one no happy man can know; and if you are alive,
and I reach home, I have still untold treasures of bliss to gather.
Oh, the joy of living with which we two will enjoy the future,
if any such is to be our lot.

"To-day we met the enemy for the first time. Up to that our
way had been through conquered territory, from which the
Danes had retreated. Smoking ruins of villages, ravaged corn-
fields, weapons and knapsacks lying about, spots where the land
was ploughed up by the shells, blood stains, bodies of horses,
trenches filled with the slain—such are the features of the scenes
through which we have been moving in the rear of the victors,
in order, if possible, to add more victories to the account— i.e.,
to burn more villages, and so forth. . . . And that we have done
to-day. We have carried the position. Behind us lies a village in
flames. The inhabitants had the good luck to have quitted it
beforehand; but in the stable a horse had been forgotten. I heard
the beast in despair stamping and shrieking. Do you know what
I did? It will procure me no decoration most certainly; for, instead of bringing down a Dane or two, I rushed to the stable
to set the poor horse free. Impossible; the manger had already
caught fire, then the straw under his hoofs, then his mane. So I
put two revolver bullets through his head. He fell down dead,
and was saved from the pain of being burned to death. Then,
back into the fight, the deathly smell of the powder, the wild
alarm of the whistling bullets, falling buildings, savage war-
cries. Most of those around me, friends and foes, were, it is true,
seized by the delirium of battle; but I remained in unblessed
sobriety. I could not get myself up to hate the Danes. They are
brave men, and what did they do but their duty in attacking us?

My thoughts were with you, Martha! I saw you laid out on your bier, and what I wished for myself was that the bullet might strike me. But at intervals, nevertheless, a ray of longing and of hope would shine again, 'What if she is alive? What if I should get home again?'

"The butchery lasted more than two hours, and we remained as I said, in possession of the field. The routed enemy fled. We did not pursue. We had work enough to do on the field. A hundred paces distant from the village stood a large farm-house, with many empty dwelling-rooms and stables; here we were to rest for the night and hither we have brought our wounded. The burial of the dead is to be done to-morrow morning. Some of the living will, of course, be shovelled in with them, for the 'stiff cramp' after a severe wound is a common phenomenon. Many who have remained out, whether dead or wounded, or even unwounded, we are obliged to abandon entirely, especially those who are lying under the ruins of the fallen houses. There they may, if dead, moulder slowly where they are; if wounded, bleed slowly to death; if unwounded, die slowly of famine. And we, hurrah! may go on with our jolly, joyous war!

"The next engagement will probably be a general action. According to all appearances there will be two entire *corps d'armée* opposed to each other. The number of the killed and wounded may in that case easily rise to 10,000; for when the cannons begin their work of vomiting out death the front ranks on both sides are soon wiped out. It is certainly a wonderful contrivance. But still better would it be if the science of artillery could progress to such a point that any army could fire a shot which would smash the whole army of the enemy at one blow. Then, perhaps, all waging of war would be entirely given up. Force would then, provided the total power of the two combatants were equally great, no longer be looked to for the solution of questions of right.

"Why am I writing all this to you? Why do I not break out, as a warrior should, into exalted hymns of triumph over our warlike work? Why? Because I thirst after truth, and after its expression without any reserve; because at all times I hate lying phrases; but at this moment, when I am so near death myself, and am speaking to you who, perhaps, are yourself lying in the death-agony, it presses on me doubly to speak what is in my heart. Even though a thousand others should think differently, or should hold themselves bound at least to speak differently, I will, nay, I *must* say it once more before I fall a sacrifice to war—I hate war. If only every man who feels the same would dare to proclaim it aloud, what a threatening protest would be shouted out to heaven! All the hurrahs which are now resounding, and all the cannon-thunder that accompanies them, would then be drowned by the battle-cry of humanity panting after humanity, by the victorious cry denouncing 'war on war'.

"Half-past three in the morning. I wrote the above last night. Then I lay down on a sack of straw and slept for an hour or two. We shall break up in half-an-hour, and then I shall be able to give this to the field-post. All is stirring now and getting ready for the march. Poor fellows! they have got little rest since the bloody work accomplished yesterday: little refreshment for that which is to be accomplished to-day. I began with a turn round our improvised field-hospital, which is to remain here. There I saw among the wounded and dying a pair for whom I would gladly have done the same as for the horse in the fire—put a bullet as a *coup de grâce* through their heads. One was a man who had had his whole lower jaw shot away, and the other— but enough. I cannot help him. Nothing can but Death. Unfortunately he is often so slow. If a man calls in despair for him he stands deaf before him. On the other hand, he is far too busy in snatching those away who with all their heart are hoping to recover, and calling on him beseechingly: 'Oh, spare me, for I have a beloved wife pining for me at home!' My horse is saddled, so now I must close these lines. Farewell, Martha, if you are still here!"

(pp. 152-5)

I succeeded in moving Frederick to the resolve of quitting the service. The circumstance that he had, after his marriage, served now more than a year, and taken a distinguished part in a campaign, would defend him from the suspicion which had occurred to my father during our engagement, that the whole marriage had for its object only to enable him to give up his career. Now, when peace should once be made, the preliminaries of which were in train, and when to all probability there were long years of peace in prospect, retirement from the army would not involve anything dishonourable. It was, indeed, still, to some extent, repugnant to Frederick's pride to give up his rank and income, and, as he said, "to do nothing, to be nothing, and to

have nothing," but his love for me was with him an even more powerful feeling than his pride, and he could not resist my entreaties. I declared that I could not go through a second time the anguish of mind which his last parting caused me; and he himself might well shrink from again calling down on us both such pain. The feeling of delicacy, which before his marriage with me, made him shrink from the idea of living on the fortune of a rich woman, no longer came into play, for we had become so completely *one* that there was no longer any perceptible difference between "mine" and "yours," and we understood each other so well that no misjudgment of his character on my part was any longer to be feared. The last campaign had besides so greatly increased his aversion to the murderous duties of war, and his unqualified expression of that aversion had so rooted it in him, that his retirement got to appear not like a concession made to our domestic happiness so much as the putting into action of his own intention, as a tribute to his convictions, and so he promised me in the coming autumn, if the negotiations for peace were then concluded, to take his discharge.
(pp. 169–70)

Above all things unbearable to me were the soldiers' games which not only my father but my brother carried on with the boy. The idea of "enemy" and "cutting down" were thus instilled into him, I know not how. One day Frederick and I came up as Rudolf was mercilessly beating two whimpering young dogs with a riding-switch.

"That is a lying Italian," he said, laying on to one of the poor beasts, "and that," on the other, "an impudent Dane."

Frederick snatched the switch out of the hand of this national corrector.

"And that is a cruel Austrian," he said, letting one or two good blows fall on Rudolf's shoulders. The Italian and the Dane gladly ran off, and the whimpering was now done by our little countryman.

"You are not angry with me, Martha, for striking your son? I am not, it is true, in favour generally of corporal punishment, but cruelty to animals provokes me."

"You did right," I said.

"Then is it only to men . . . that one may . . . be cruel?" asked the boy between his sobs.

"Oh, no; still less."

"But you, yourself, have hit Italians and Danes."

"They were enemies."

"Then one *may* hate them?"

(p. 171)

Up to this time I had had tidings regularly. Though in his first letter he had prepared me for his being able only to write little, yet Frederick had made use of every opportunity to send me a word or two. In pencil, on horseback, in his tent, in a hasty scrawl only legible by me, he would write on pages torn out of his note-book letters destined for me. Some he found opportunities for sending, and some did not come into my hands till the campaign was over.

I have kept these memorials up to the present hour. They are not careful, polished descriptions of the war, such as the war correspondents of the papers offer in their despatches, or the historians of the war in their publications; no sketches of battles worked up with all the technicalities of strategical details; no battle-pictures heightened with rhetorical flights, in which the narrator is always occupied in letting his own imperturbility, heroism, and patriotic enthusiasm shine out. Frederick's sketches are nothing of this sort, I know. But what they are, I need not decide. Here are some of them :—

*　　*　　*

"The village is ours—no, it is the enemy's—now ours again—and yet once more the enemy's; but it is no longer a village, but a smoking mass of the ruins of houses.

"The inhabitants (was it not really *their* village?) had left it previously and were away—luckily for them, for the fighting in an inhabited place is something really fearful; for then the bullets from friend and foe fall into the midst of the rooms and kill women and children. One family, however, had remained behind in the place which yesterday we took, lost, re-took, and lost again—namely, an old married couple and their daughter, the latter in childbed. The husband is serving in our regiment. He told me the story as we were nearing the village. 'There, colonel, in that house with the red roof, is living my wife with her old parents. They have not been able to get away, poor creatures; my wife may be confined any moment, and the old

folks are half-crippled; for God's sake, colonel, order me there!'
Poor devil! he got there just in time to see the mother and child
die; a shell had exploded under their bed. What has happened
to the old folks I do not know. They are probably buried under
the ruins; the house was one of the first set on fire by the
cannonade. Fighting in the open country is terrible enough, but
fighting amongst human dwellings is ten times more cruel. Crashing timber, bursting flames, stifling smoke; cattle run mad with
fear; every wall a fortress or a barricade, every window a shot-
hole. I saw a breastwork there which was formed of corpses. The
defenders had heaped up all the slain that were lying near, in
order, from that rampart, to fire over on to their assailants. I
shall surely never forget that wall in all my life. A man, who
formed one of its bricks, penned in among the other corpse-
bricks, was still alive, and was moving his arm.

" 'Still alive'—that is a condition, occurring in war with a
thousand differences, which conceals sufferings incalculable. If
there were any angel of mercy hovering over the battlefields he
would have enough to do in giving the poor creatures—men and
beasts—who are 'still alive' their *coup de grâce*."

*   *   *

"Another day of marching, with one or two skirmishes. I have
experienced a great sorrow. Such a mournful picture accompanies me. Among the many pictures of woe which are all
around me this ought not so to strike me, ought not to give me
such pain. But I cannot help it; it touches me nearly, and I cannot shake it off. Puxl—our poor, happy, good, little dog—oh, if
I had only left him at home with his little master, Rudolf! He
was running after us, as usual. Suddenly he gave a shriek of pain;
the splinter of a shell had torn off his fore-leg. He could not come
after us, so is left behind, and is 'still alive'. Between twenty-four
and forty-eight hours have passed, and he is 'still alive'. 'Oh
master! my good master!' his cries seemed to say. 'Do not leave
poor Puxl here! His heart will break!' And what especially pains
me is the thought that the faithful dying creature must misunder-
stand me. For he saw that I turned round, that I must have
understood his cry for help and yet was so cold and so cruel as to
leave him there. Poor Puxl could not understand that a regiment
advancing to the attack, out of whose ranks comrades are falling
and are left on the ground, cannot be ordered to halt for the
sake of a dog who has been hit. He has no conception of the

11—SFP * *

higher duty which I had to obey : and so the poor true heart of the dog is complaining of my unmercifulness. Only think of troubling oneself about such trumpery in the midst of the 'great events' and gigantic misfortunes which fill the present time. That is what many would say, with a shrug of the shoulders; but not you, Martha, not you. I know that a tear will come into your eyes for our poor Puxl."

*   *   *

"What is all I have seen to-day? If I shut my eyes, what has passed before them comes with terrible distinctness into my memory. 'Nothing but pain and pictures of horror,' you will say. Why then do other men bring such fresh, such joyful images away with them from war? Ah, yes! These others close their eyes to the pain and the horror. They *say nothing about them.* If they write, or if they narrate, they give themselves no trouble to paint their experiences after nature; but they occupy themselves in imitating descriptions which they have read, and which they take as models, and in bringing out those impressions which are considered heroic. If they occasionally tell also of scenes of destruction, which contain in themselves the bitterest pain and the bitterest terror, nothing of either is to be discovered in their tone. On the contrary, the more terrible the more indifferent are they, the more horrible the more easy. Disapprobation, anger, excitement? Nothing of all this. Well, perhaps instead of this, a slight breath of sentimental pity, a few sighs of compassion. But their heads are soon in the air again. 'The heart to God, and the hand against the foe.' Hurrah, Tra-ra-ra !

"Now look at two of the pictures which impressed themselves on me.

"Steep, rocky heights. Jägers nimble as cats climbing up them. The object was to 'take' the heights, from the top of which the enemy was firing. What I see are the forms of the assailants who are climbing up, and some of them who are hit by the enemy's shot, suddenly stretch both arms out, let their muskets fall, and with their heads falling backwards, drop off the height, step by step, from one rocky point to another, smashing their limbs to pieces.

"I see a horseman at some distance obliquely behind me, at whose side a shell burst. His horse swerved aside, and came against the tail of mine, then shot past me. The man sat still in the saddle, but a fragment of the shell had ripped his belly open, and torn all the intestines out. The upper part of his body was held on to the lower only by the spine. From the ribs to the thighs nothing but one great bleeding cavity. A short distance further he fell to the ground, with one foot still clinging in the stirrup, and the galloping horse dragging him on over the stony soil."

*   *   *

"It is decided—if I come back from this campaign, I quit the service. Setting everything else aside, if one has learned to regard anything with such horror as war produces in me, it would be a continual lie to keep in the service of that thing. Even before this, I went, as you know, to battle unwillingly, and with a judgment condemnatory of it; but now this unwillingness has so increased, this condemnation has become so strengthened, that all the reasons which before determined me to persevere with my profession have ceased to operate. The sentiments derived from my youthful training, and perhaps also, to some extent, inherited, which still pleaded with me in favour of the military life, have now quite departed from me in the course of the horrors I have just experienced. I do not know whether it is the studies which I undertook in common with you, and from which I discovered that my contempt for war is not an isolated feeling, but is shared by the best spirits of the age, or whether it is the conversations I have had with you, in which I have strengthened myself in my views by their free expression and your concurrence in them; in one word, my former vague, half-smothered feeling has changed into a clear conviction, a conviction which makes it from this time impossible to do service to the war god. It is the same kind of change as comes to many people in matters of belief. First they are somewhat sceptical and indifferent, still they can assist at the business of the temple with a certain sense of reverence. But when once all mysticism is put aside, when they rise to the perception that the ceremony which they are attending rests on folly, and sometimes on cruel folly, as in the case of the religious death-sacrifices, then they will no longer kneel beside the other befooled folks, no longer deceive themselves and the world be entering the now desecrated temple. This is the process which has gone on with me in relation to the cruel worship of Mars. The mysterious, supernatural, awe-inspiring feeling which the appearance of this deity generally awakes in men, and which in former times obscured my senses also, has now entirely passed away for me. The liturgy of the bulletins and the ritual of heroic phraseology no longer appear to me as a divine revelation; the mighty organ-voice of the cannon, the incense-smoke of the powder have no charm more for me. I assist at the terrible worship perfectly devoid of belief or reverence, and can now see nothing in it except the tortures of the victims, hear nothing but their wailing death-cries. And thence comes it that these pages, which I am filling with my impressions of war, contain nothing except pain seen with pain."

(pp. 232–44)

The ambulance was placed behind a hillock which protected it. The battle was raging on the other side. The ground quavered, and the heated air quavered. Clouds of smoke were rising, the artillery was roaring. Now the duty was to send out patrols to repair to the scene of battle, pick out the badly wounded, and bring them in. Is there anything more heroic than such going into the midst of the hissing rain of bullets, in the face of all the horrors of the fight, exposed to all the perils of the fight, without allowing oneself to be penetrated by its wild excitement? According to military conceptions this office is not distinguished. On "the Sanitary Corps" no smart, active, handy, young fellow will serve. No man in it turns the girls' heads. And a field doctor, even if one is no longer called by that name, but "regimental surgeon," can he nevertheless hold a comparison with any cavalry lieutenant?

The corporal of the Sanitary Corps ordered his people towards some low ground against which a battery had opened its fire. They marched through the dark veil of the powder smoke and the dust and the scattered earth to a point where a cannon ball, which struck the ground at their feet, bounded in front of them. They had only gone a few paces when they began to meet with wounded men, men slightly wounded, who were crawling to the ambulance, either alone or in pairs, giving each other mutual support. One sank down; but it was not his wounds which had sapped his strength, it was exhaustion. "We have eaten nothing for two days, made a forced march of twelve hours, got into the bivouac, and then, two hours afterwards, came the alarm and the fight."

The patrol went forward. These men would find their way for

themselves, and manage to take their exhausted comrade with them. Aid must be reserved for others still more in need of aid.

On a heap of rocks, forming part of a precipitous declivity, lies a bleeding mass. There are a dozen soldiers lying there. The sanitary corporal stops and bandages one or two of them. But these wounded men are not carried off; those must first be fetched in who have fallen in the centre of the field. Then, perhaps, on their return march, these men can be picked up here.

And again the patrol goes on, nearer to the battle. In ever thicker swarms wounded men are tottering on, painfully creeping forward, singly or together. These are such as can still walk. The contents of the field flasks is distributed amongst these, a bandage is applied to such wounds as are bleeding, and the way to the ambulance pointed out to them. Then forward again. Over the dead—over hillocks of corpses. Many of these dead show traces of horrible agonies. Eyes staring unnaturally, hands grasping the ground, the hair of the beard staring out, teeth pressed together, lips closed spasmodically, legs stiffly outstretched. So they lie.

Now through a hollow way. Here they are lying in heaps, dead and wounded together. The latter greet the sanitary patrol as angels of rescue, and beg and shriek for help. With broken voices, weeping and lamenting, they shout for rescue, for a gulp of water. But alas! the provisions are almost exhausted, and what can these few men do? Each ought to have a hundred arms to be able to rescue them all. Yet each does what he can. Then sounds the prolonged tone of the sanitary call. The men stop and break off from their work of aid. "Do not desert us! Do not desert us!" the poor injured men cry; but the signal horn calls again and again, and this, plainly distinguishable from all other noises, is evidently going further afield. Then also an adjutant comes in hot haste. "Men of the Sanitary Corps?" "At your command," replies the corporal. "Follow me."

Evidently a general wounded. It is necessary to obey and leave the rest. "Patience, comrades, and keep a good heart; we will return." Those who hear and those who say it know that it is not true.

And again they go further: following the adjutant, at the double quick, who spurs on in front and points the way. There is no halting on the way, although on the right hand and on the left resound shrieks of woe and cries for help; and although also many bullets fall among those who are thus hurrying on, and stretch one and another on the ground—only onwards and over everything. Over men writhing with the pain of their wounds, men trodden down by horses tearing over them, or crushed by guns passing over their limbs, and who, seeing the rescue corps, mutilated as they are, rear themselves up for the last time. Over them, over them!

(pp. 252–4)

"Calm yourself, dear Tilling. You are a genuine faddist. If you could only point me out a means to do away with war it would be a perfect benefit, to be sure. But as that is not possible, every nation must surely endeavour to prepare itself for it as well as possible, in order to assure itself of the greatest chance of winning in the inevitable 'struggle for existence'—that is the cant word of the fashionable Darwinism, is it not?"

"If I should choose to suggest to you the means of doing away with wars, you would again call me a silly faddist, a sentimental dreamer rendered morbid by the 'humanitarian craze'—that, I think, is the cant word in favour with the war party, is it not?"

"To be sure, I cannot conceal from you that no practical foundation exists for the realisation of such an ideal. One must calculate with the actual factors. In these are classed the passions of men; their rivalries; the divergences of interests; the impossibility of coming to an agreement on all questions."

"But that is not necessary. When disagreements begin an arbitration tribunal—not force—is to decide."

"The sovereign states would never betake themselves to such a tribunal—nor would the peoples."

"The peoples? The potentates and diplomatists would not—but the people? Just inquire, and you will find that the wish for peace is warm and true in the people, while the peaceful assurances which proceed from the governments are frequently lies, hypocritical lies—or at least are regarded as such on principle by other governments. That is precisely what is called 'diplomacy'. And the peoples will go on ever more and more calling for peace. If the general obligation of defence should extend, the dislike of war will increase in the same proportion. A class of soldiers animated with love for their calling is, of course, imaginable; their exceptional position, which they take for a position of honour, is offered to them as a recompense for the sacrifices which it entails, but when the exception ceases the distinction ceases also. The admiring thankfulness disappears which those

who stay at home offer to those who go out in their defence,—
because then there will be no one to stay at home. The war-
loving feelings which are always being suggested to the soldier—
and in so doing are often awakened in him—will be more seldom
kindled; for who are those that are of the most heroic spirit, who
are most warm in their enthusiasm for the exploits and dangers
of war? Those who are safe against them—the professors, the
politicians, the beer-shop chatterers—the chorus of old men, as
it is called in 'Faust'. When the safety is lost, that chorus will be
silenced. Besides, if not only those devote themselves to the military life who love and praise it, but all those also are forcibly
dragged into it who look on it with horror, that horror must
work. Poets, thinkers, friends of humanity, timid persons, all
these will, from their own points of view, curse the trade they are
forced into."

"But they will beyond doubt have to keep silent about this
way of thinking, in order not to pass for cowards—in order not
to expose themselves to the displeasure of the higher powers."

"Keep silence? Not for ever. As I talk—though I have myself
kept silence long—so will the others also break out into speech.
If the thought ripens, the word will come. I am an individual
who have come to the age of forty before my conviction
acquired sufficient strength to expand itself in words. And as I
have required two or three decades, so the masses will perhaps
require two or three generations—but speak they will at last."

(pp. 353–5)

Many of the previous pages have I written with shuddering
and with self-compulsion. It was not without inward horror that
I could describe the scenes through which I passed in my journey
to Bohemia, and the cholera week at Grumitz. I have done it in
order to obey my sense of duty. Beloved lips once gave me the
solemn command : "In case I die before you, you must take my
task in hand and labour for the work of Peace". If this binding
injunction had not been laid on me, I could never have so far
prevailed over myself as to tear open the agonised wounds of my
reminiscences so unsparingly.

Now, however, I have come to an event, which I will relate,
but which I will not, nor can I describe.

No—I cannot, I cannot!

I have tried—ten half-written torn pages are lying on the

floor by the side of my writing-table—but a heart-pang seized me; my thoughts froze up, or got into wild entanglement in my brain, and I had to throw the pen aside and weep, bitter hot tears, with cries like a child.

Now a few hours afterwards I resume my pen. But as to describing the particulars of the next event, as to relating what I felt when it happened, I must give that up—the thing itself is sufficient.

Frederick—my own one—was, in consequence of a letter from Berlin that was found in his house, suspected of espionage—was surrounded by a mob of fanatics, crying: "*A mort—à mort le Prussien*"—dragged before a tribunal of patriots, and on February 1, 1871, shot by order of a court-martial.
(pp. 418–19)

To-day there is hardly any one left who has not dreamed this dream, or who would not confess its beauty. And there are watchers too; watchers conspicuous enough, who are longing to awake mankind out of the long sleep of savagery, and energetically and with a single eye to their object collecting themselves for the purpose of planting the white flag. Their battle-cry is, "War on War," their watchword, the only word which can have power to deliver from ruin Europe armed against herself is, "Lay down your arms". In all places, in England and France, in Italy, in the northern countries, in Germany, in Switzerland, in America, associations have been formed, whose object is, through the compulsion of public opinion, through the commanding pressure of the people's will, to move the Governments to submit their differences in future to an Arbitration Court, appointed by themselves, and so once for all to enthrone justice in place of brute force. That this is no dream, no "enthusiasm," is proved by the facts that the questions of the Alabama, the Caroline Islands, and several others have already been settled in this manner. And it is not only people without power or position, like the poor blacksmith of a former time, who are now co-operating in this work of peace; no, members of parliament, bishops, professors, senators, ministers are inscribed on the lists. I know all this (which is unknown to most people, because I have kept in communication with all those persons, with whom Frederick established relations in the pursuit of his noble aim. What I found out, by means of these persons, about the successes and the designs of the peace societies has been duly entered in *The Protocol of Peace*. The last of these entries is the following letter which the president of the International Arbitration and Peace Association, having its headquarters in London, wrote me in answer to an inquiry bearing on this subject:—

"INTERNATIONAL ARBITRATION AND PEACE ASSOCIATION,
"LONDON, 41 OUTER TEMPLE, *July*, 1889.

"Madam,—You have honoured me by inquiring as to the actual position of the great question to which you have devoted your life. Here is my answer: At no time, perhaps, in the history of the world has the cause of peace and good-will been more hopeful. It seems that, at last, the long night of death and destruction will pass away; and we who are on the mountain-top of humanity think that we see the first streaks of the dawn on the kingdom of Heaven upon earth. It may seem strange that we should say this at a moment when the world has never seen so many armed men and such frightful engines of destruction ready for their accursed work; but when things are at their worst they begin to mend. Indeed, the very ruin which these armies are bringing in their train produces universal consternation; and soon the oppressed peoples must rise and with one voice say to their rulers: 'Save us, and save our children from the famine which awaits us, if these things continue; save civilisation and all the triumphs which the efforts of wise and great men have accomplished in its name; save the world from a return to barbarism, rapine and terror!'

" 'What indications,' do you ask, 'are there of such a dawn of a better day?' Well, let me ask in reply, is not the recent meeting at Paris of the representatives of one hundred societies for the declaration of international concord, for the substitution of a state of law and justice for that of force and wrong, an event unparalleled in history? Have we not seen men of many nations assembled on this occasion and elaborating, with enthusiasm and unanimity, practical schemes for this great end? Have we not seen, for the first time in history, a Congress of Representatives of the parliaments of free nations declaring in favour of treaties being signed by all civilised states, whereby they shall bind themselves to defer their differences to the arbitrament of equity, pronounced by an authorised tribunal instead of a resort to wholesale murder? . . ."

(pp. 425–6)

"To be sure," began the Minister thoughtfully; and again Lori Griesbach turned her eyes on him with admiration. "To be sure, it would be a fine thing if a unanimous vote in favour of laying down one's arms could be brought about; but, on the other side, what Government would dare to make the beginning? To be sure, there is nothing so desirable as concord; but, on the other side, how can lasting concord be thought possible so long as human passions, separate interests, and so forth, still continue?"

"I beg your pardon," said my son Rudolf, now taking the word. "Forty millions of inhabitants in a state form one whole. Then why not several hundred millions? Can this be susceptible of logical and mathematical proof, that so long as human passions, separate interests, and so forth, still continue, it is indeed possible for forty millions of people to renounce the right to go to war with each other about them; nay, three states, like the present triple alliance, may ally themselves together, and form a 'League of Peace'; but five states cannot do it, and must not do it. Truly, truly, our world of to-day gives itself out as wondrous wise, and laughs at the savages; and yet in many things we also cannot count up to five."

Some voices made themselves heard: "What?" "Savages?" "That about us, with our over-refined culture?" "At the end of the nineteenth century?"

Rudolf stood up.

"Yes; savages. I will not recall the word. And so long as we cling to the past we shall remain savages. But we are already standing at the gate of a new period. Glances are directed forwards. All are pressing on strongly towards another, a higher form. Savagery, with its idols and its weapons—there are many who are already edging away gradually from it. If even we may be nearer to barbarism than most people believe, we are also perhaps nearer to our ennoblement than most people hope. *The prince or statesman is perhaps already alive* who is to bring to perfection the exploit which will live in all future history as the most glorious and most enlightened of all exploits—that which will carry universal disarmament. We have placed our feet already on the threshold of an age in which manhood is to raise itself into humanity—to the nobility of humanity, as Frederick Tilling used to say. Mother, I drink this glass now to the memory of your unforgotten, loved, and trusted one, to whom I too owe everything, all I think and all I am; and from that glass (and he threw it against the wall, where it shattered to pieces) shall no other drop ever be drunk again; and to-day, at my new-born child's christening, shall no other toast be proposed than *this*— 'Hail to the future!' To fulfil its tasks shall we clothe ourselves in steel? No. Shall we endeavour to show ourselves worthy of our fathers' fathers, as the old phrase goes? No. But of our grandsons' grandsons. Mother," said he, breaking off, "you are weeping. What is the matter with you? What do you see there?"

My gaze had been directed to the open glass door. The rays of the setting sun had thrown a halo of tremulous gold round a rose-bush, and from this, rising up in life-like clearness, was my dream-picture. I saw the garden-shears glitter, the white hair shine. He smiled at me as he said, "Are we not a happy old couple?"

Ah, woe is me!

Finis

(tr. T. Holmes)

(pp. 434-5)

MEMORIES OF ALFRED NOBEL

"Do I, figuratively speaking, possess a heart? . . . That I do not know, but this much is certain, that in the physiological sense that organ of mine is greviously ill." Such were the words Alfred Nobel, with whom I had been in friendly contact for over twenty years, directed to me in his last letter to me, a week before his sudden death.

The magnificent provisions of his will leave us in no doubt of the fact that he had a heart, a great heart which was capable of encompassing the whole of mankind, and not just the men of today, but also the generations to come, those who were to find themselves raised to the level of true civilisation by the achievements of science, and the ideals of art and peace.

In his last years Alfred Nobel regularly made donations to the Austrian Peace Society, and whenever this fact was made public his detractors never failed to point out the paradox of a man who had invented dynamite and progressive smokeless powder being a peace fanatic. No, he was no "fanatic", he was working resolutely and clearheadedly towards peace. The sums of money he received from the arms race he set aside for the advancement of human knowledge. And, as Pasteur said in his jubilee speech at the Sorbonne, it will be knowledge which will ultimately conquer war. When, some little while ago, Nobel made a grant of 80,000 francs to the aeronaut Andrée, who wanted to make the north polar journey by balloon, he wrote to me: "You see, this is yet another way of helping the cause of peace, for every new discovery leaves its traces in men's spirits which makes it possible for ever more men in the next generation to emerge who are capable of redefining civilisation in ever higher terms."

Nobel also worked on unceasingly towards the perfection of weapons and projectiles. The increasing horror of the weapons of war could, in his view, only make the absurdity and impossibility of war in the future ever more apparent and thus contribute to the end of war.

At first this was the only way, and a somewhat indirect one at that, in which he worked towards the achievement of peace among the nations: on the one hand, doing away with man's folly and brutality through the medium of art and science, the elimination of suffering by the advancement of a consumer-based technology; and on the other hand, the achievement of a *reductio ad absurdum* of war by increasing its terrible potential. It took Alfred Nobel a very long time to come to recognise that there was also a straighter and more direct path to the achievement of international peace, namely the establishment of organisations working towards this specific goal. When we met by chance in Bern in the summer of 1892, when the peace congress was actually in session, he still knew as good as nothing about the movement. I explained to him everything about its methods and objectives. "If I came to be convinced," he told me, "that these organisations are a more rapid means of attaining the goal of peace I should set a large sum aside for them—but first I must hear all the facts of the matter." And since that time he remained in constant contact with the movement and always had accurate information about its progress and achievements.

It was a rare intellectual privilege indeed to converse with Alfred Nobel about the world and man, about art and life, the problems of time and eternity. His conversation was sparkling yet profound, and the perfection with which this Swede mastered spoken and written German, French and English was little short of miraculous—he was so thoroughly versed in every subtle shade of idiom that one might have taken any one of these three languages for his mother tongue. When my husband and I were in Paris in the winter of 1887, we passed many a stimulating hour in his charming little "hôtel" in the Avenue Malakoff. The small company would foregather in his study, which was situated on the ground floor. It was a very simply furnished room. A large writing desk, a bookcase, a few leather upholstered chairs were the only furniture, but there was one valuable decoration in the shape of a Munkacsy painting which hung above the sofa. The bookcase contained only the works of philosophers and poets. Byron's complete works occupied the place of honour; and Nobel could quote whole pages by heart from his favourite poet. Next door there was the chemical laboratory. A hurried glance in there was enough. The manufacture of dynamite and other similar means of world destruction was something which did not really belong in a home. Then we moved upstairs to a quite exquisite dinner. Although a man of very simple tastes himself, Nobel delighted in placing before his guests the most delightful and exotic delicacies; fruit, for example—direct from Africa, things which up to then we had only known by name, and also the rarest vintages of Chateau Yquem and Johannisberger, while he himself drank a little "coloured water". Black coffee was served in a little conservatory which adjoined on to the dining room. In this little palace, everything was in miniature, even the green reception room with its malachite furniture, and next to it a tiny little music room, furnished in red and lit with subdued red lighting.

As a hard-working, but somewhat solitary man he did not receive many guests and only rarely appeared in society. He was repelled by the empty gossiping of the salons, and there was in general more than a touch of scorn, bitterness and mistrust against real people for all his great love for the abstract ideals of humanity. Certain kinds of insipidity, superstition and frivolity filled him with an almost angry repugnance. His life was centred on his books, his studies and his experiments. And it probably caused his early death too, for he permitted himself no rest, but worked on physically and intellectually without let-up. He would often travel early in the morning to his laboratories two miles from Paris and remain there until evening, only interrupting his work for a cold snack which he had taken with him.

We met Nobel for the last time in Switzerland in 1892; although we have not seen him since then, we continue our lively correspondence. In Switzerland he invited my husband and myself to be his guests in Zurich for a couple of days.

There he used to spend a little while every year in the Hotel Bauer by the lake. For us he had taken the rooms which the Empress Elizabeth, who had stayed over in Zurich for several days as she was journeying through, had left the day before. It was the end of September, and I shall never forget the most beautiful autumn weather that accompanied our trip on the Lake of Zurich on board one of Nobel's own craft made of— aluminium. The elegantly built boat glided like a shimmering toy over the surface of the water which itself shimmered like silver. It had no sail, no steam engine, only a tiny petrol motor, and the crew consisted of a single engineer, who was at one and the same time the captain, navigator and cabin-boy of this pleasure yacht.

The three of us conversed about war and peace and how beautiful God's world could be if the divine spark, which glows in the hearts and minds of many men but which is still choked by ignorance and brutality, caught into flame.

Alfred Nobel and I agreed there and then to collaborate on a book, a campaigning book against all that is base in the world, and we had got as far as discussing the title. But like many such projects, this did not come to fulfilment.

If this gifted man had not been a great inventor he would have attained a high level as a creative writer; he would himself have achieved that "literary product with idealist tendencies" which he seeks to inspire in the writers of the future through his endowment. I have read poems of his in manuscript—as far as I know none of them have ever been published—written in English which in places match their English model Byron in both breadth and depth. A few months ago, when he had already been sick for some time, he wrote to me that, since illness had impeded his professional work, he had used his enforced idleness to complete a drama, *Beatrice Cenci*. I asked him to let me read the play, but he replied that he had written it in Swedish and had as yet not translated it.

Whether or not his drama, poems or philosophical works are found among his papers after his death and published, he has none the less composed a masterpiece of immeasurable significance : namely, his will. Not because he gives millions away, not because he sets up foundations to reward scientific discoveries, but because in it he expresses an entirely new form of beneficence : instead of advancing the cause of current and future suffering, he rewards steps taken towards the removal of future suffering. Nobel, in drawing up his will, had a vision of ennobling human society : the world was to be made the richer and more beautiful by new discoveries, new knowledge, and idealistic works of art, and to make all these things secure there was one basic precondition : peace.

THE NEXT PEACE CONGRESS IN ROME

This is the way things stand: armies of millions, divided into two camps, rattling their weapons, just waiting for the signal to hurl themselves at one another's throats. Only the mutual fear and trembling at the unutterable horror of the threatening storm has been some kind of guarantee that the storm will not break. But postponing a threat is not the same thing as removing it altogether. The so-called "blessings" of peace which this state of armed fear is striving to preserve are only guaranteed to us on a short-term basis, as lasting perhaps no more than for a little while longer. The powers joined in armed alliance for the "preservation of the peace" will have nothing to do with the abolition of war itself, of renunciation of the principle of balance of force. For them, war is sacred, something that cannot be abolished, and one should not seek to wish it out of existence; but at the same time they regard it as a terrible thing, because of the proportions a future conflagration might assume, a thing not to be had on one's conscience, and thus something one must not be instrumental in starting. But what kind of unnatural thing is this that can neither stop nor begin, can neither be affirmed nor denied? Is it unceasing preparation for an eventuality which will be avoided by the act of preparation itself, and at the same time the avoidance of an eventuality whose coming is prepared for by avoiding it? This monstrous paradox can be explained as follows: the image of war we have inherited from the past—and which people are still anxious to keep alive—as a "glad-hearted and spirited" campaign that changes boundaries and bestows power without involving more than a fraction of the population has, as a result of the way our civilisation has advanced, become a physical and moral impossibility. Morally impossible, because man has lost his savagery and scorn for human life, physically impossible, because the increasing sophistication of the techniques of mass destruction over the past twenty years will turn the next military campaign into something quite new, something quite different, which it will no longer be possible to designate by the name of war. If you took several hours preparing a bath, heating the water hotter and hotter until it boiled—would anyone stepping, or rather, falling into it still call it a "bath"? A few more years of such "maintained" peace, of such inventions of machines of destruction—electrical mines, aerial torpedoes loaded with explosives—and on the day war breaks out they will all be blown to eternity: double, triple, quadruple alliances and the rest.

The explosion could come at any moment. Those who hold the fuse in their hands are fortunately paying heed. They know that with such stockpiles of powder the consequences would be frightful if they lit the fuse negligently or, worse, with criminal intent. And in order to intensify this benevolent caution the stocks of powder are increased still further. Would it not be simpler for all to agree freely to dispense with the fuse itself? In other words, to disarm? To institute a system of international justice, to bring the divided power groupings into a single federation, to prevent aggression from resulting in mutual conflict—in other words, to found a league of the civilised states of Europe? The various alliances stand opposed to one another, in a state of balance of power and status. What can prevent them from making their claimed goal—peace—into the basis for a single alliance? What can prevent them? The law of inertia on the one hand and on the other the flames of national hatred which the most vocal party in every country—the proponents of war—are constantly fanning. Perhaps the most vocal, but also the smallest. Little knots of chauvinists scattered here and there. In Russia a clique of Pan-Slavists—the Czar wants peace; in France a group of revanchists—the government wants peace; in Austria and in Germany a handful of militarists—both Kaisers want peace. Let alone the common people—they long for peace, and have a right to peace. The cries of comradeship in arms, which are shouted out now and again when the various fleets exchange greetings and which can so easily be interpreted as an expression of the martial aspirations of the people, should no longer be so misunderstood; will people never learn that there is nothing more infectious than cheering and shouting—that such cries inevitably are heard the moment after the first signal is given, whatever the cause—that they follow like thunder upon lightning?

There is no doubt that those who actively seek war are in a tiny minority. Even smaller are the numbers of those who loudly make open admission of such views. By contrast, the masses of those who long for peace are immeasurably vast—real guaranteed peace, not a nervous provisional state of non-war. Anyone holding on high the white banner of peace will be followed by people in their millions. But among those millions the numbers are also small of those who have banded together to proclaim their objectives and to work together towards peace.

But not so few as many might believe. In recent years the peace movement has gained undreamed-of impetus and breadth. This international organisation has drawn its supporters from all areas of the population, as well as among the most notable of the powerful and influential classes. It is a well-known fact that, although they have not actually joined the international movement, the whole social democrat movement has adopted the identical aims of "disarmament and courts of arbitration" as part of its programme; and in addition permanent peace associations have been formed in the various European parliaments with the object of taking the resolutions passed in the interparliamentary and placing them before their own governments. One such proposal which was brought before the Italian chamber by R. Bonghi and signed also by the later premier di Rudini is particularly noteworthy.

Practically every European parliament will be sending delegates to the next conference. (For this purpose the Norwegian Storting has set aside 3,000 Kroner for the travelling expenses of three delegates.) About seventy French deputies will be represented. The invitations were issued by the Italian chamber, and of these three hundred—more than half of the elected representatives—are members of the "Comitato permanente della Pace".

Alongside this conference attended only by politicians the great international congress will take place in which delegates of all the existing peace societies will participate. And Rome is preparing a worthy welcome for them too. The committee which has come into being to prepare and run the congress has been divided into three sections, headed by the Vice-President of the senate, Marquis Alfieri, the President of the privy council, senator Cadorni, and member of the house Prince Ruspoli. In the presence of all the officials, the congress will be solemnly opened on Monday 9 November at three o'clock in the afternoon in the Capitol. The sessions that follow will be held in the hall of the press association. The city will put on some special events for the members of the congress, among others a reception by the Mayor of Rome in the Capitoline museum, an excursion by special train to Naples and Pompeii, and the festive illumination of the Forum and the Colosseum.

It can readily be anticipated that these occasions will represent an imposing demonstration on behalf of the principle of international justice originating in Rome and finding an echo throughout the whole of the rest of Europe—louder, it is to be hoped, than the voices of incitement and defiance which have in the past disturbed our corner of the globe. If the hounds of war, which fear has up to now kept in restraint, despite the fact that they are straining at the leash, are not let loose, if the present state of preparation for war—for it can hardly be called peace—can be maintained for another two or three years, then it is possible that the days spent in Rome and the future work that is set in train there, that next year's congress, to be held in Vienna perhaps or Berlin, or the one planned for Chicago's exhibition year, for which the invitations are to go out to European governments directly from President Harrison himself, possible, that all these things will enable civilised man to avert the monstrous disaster in good time and of his own free will, which will otherwise inevitably burst upon us. Only then will it be possible for a new age to dawn, freed from barbarity.

But if this aspiration is to be fulfilled, if the will of the people to peace and harmony is to be mobilised, then it is essential that it should find its voice. For this reason it is vital that, wherever supporters of peace exist, they should make open confession of their beliefs and to the very limits of their ability work actively for the cause. In many cases the mere use of a name can have a considerable effect. It is beyond question that there are innumerable people in Vienna and in Austria as a whole who support the objectives of the Rome congress, but they have not come together, there is no Austrian branch of the international league; and if none appears before next November Russia and Austro-Hungary would find themselves the only two civilised countries in Europe unrepresented at the congress. This would cause people to come to the entirely false and highly damaging conclusion that we do not want international peace. It is true that in the Austrian house of representatives a group of supporters has come together which has agreed to support the interparliamentary conference, and that in itself is of great value; but it is not enough. For them in particular, as emissaries of the people, it is essential that they do not make their appearance in isolation, but have behind them a broad section of the population, which can make its presence felt at the conference that follows on the congress (and which parliamentarians and statesmen will attend) and which can then carry out according to plan their allotted tasks of propaganda, influencing the education of the young, involving the press and the pulpit, uninterrupted contacts with other peace societies, and more besides.

A start has already been made, but this matter must be settled some few weeks before the opening of the congress. I now request all those who wish to participate to send in their name and address, to the address of the writer, who has been officially empowered by the controlling committee of the Rome congress to make this appeal to her fellow countrymen and women.

THE DEVELOPMENT OF THE PEACE MOVEMENT

The eternal truths and rights have always lain dormant within the human spirit, but only in the fullness of time are they aroused, filled with life, translated into deeds.

One of these truths is that peace is the basis and objective of happiness, and one of these rights is the right to one's own life. The strongest of all human drives, the drive towards self-preservation, is a proof of this right's existence, and it has been solemnly recognised in the form of an age-old commandment which runs : "Thou shalt not kill."

But at the present stage of human cultural development how little that law is respected and that commandment followed I do not need to tell you. The whole military structure of our social order depends upon denial of the opportunities of peace, contempt for human life and the lust to kill.

And because this is so, and has been so for the few thousand years—such a short period of time—of our world history, many indeed most people believe that it will always be like that. There is far too little recognition of the fact that the world is constantly changing and developing, for the discovery of the law of evolution itself belongs to the recent past of our scientific development, although it dominates all life.

No; faith in the continuing permanence of the past and the present is a mistaken belief. Past and present flow past on the tide of time like some shoreline; and the ship laden with mankind is borne along on the current towards ever new shores, towards the future.

Those who have recognised the law of evolution and seek to advance its operation are convinced that what is to come is always a degree better, nobler, happier than what lies in the past. Only by recognition and conscious application of the laws and forces of nature, both on the physical and moral planes, will those technical discoveries and social institutions be created which will ease, enrich and ennoble our lives. Such things are designated as ideal for as long as they remain in the realm of the idea, but they stand before us as concrete achievements as soon as they have been brought into visible, living and viable form.

"If you keep me in touch and I discover that the peace movement is beginning to embark on the road towards practical implementation, then I shall help it on its way with financial assistance."

Those are the words of the noble Scandinavian, to whom I owe the honour, ladies and gentlemen, of being able to speak to you today—words addressed to me in 1892 by Alfred Nobel in Bern, where he met my husband and myself during the course of the peace congress there.

Alfred Nobel's will gives ample evidence of the fact that he gradually convinced himself that the movement had come down out of the clouds of pious theorising to the solid ground of attainable goals marked out in practical terms. Alongside the other factors which he designated as contributory to the advancement of civilised society, namely science and idealist literature, he placed the goals of the peace congress, namely, the achievement of international system of justice and a consequent reduction in armed forces.

Alfred Nobel too was of the opinion that social changes only take place slowly and indirectly. He had donated 80,000 francs to Andrée's north polar expedition. He wrote to me about it that it would be of far greater service to the cause of peace than I would credit.

"If Andrée reaches his goal, even if he only achieves half of what he sets out to attain, this will be one of those successes which will set in motion that din and excitement which inspire men's spirits and bring about the creation and adoption of new ideas and new reforms."

But Nobel also saw before him a nearer and more direct path. On a different occasion he wrote to me :

"Men could and should soon arrive at the conclusion that all states must come together and agree to engage in joint hostilities against any aggressor state. That would render war impossible and would compel even the most brutal and irrational power either to turn to the court of arbitration or to hold its peace. If the Triple Alliance embraced all states, instead of just three, then peace would be guaranteed for centuries."

Alfred Nobel did not live to see the great advances and the decisive series of events which have led to the idea of peace being translated into real terms, that is, functioning institutions.

But in 1894 he was able to know that the great English statesman Gladstone went further than the principle of a court of arbitration and proposed the institution of a standing international tribunal. A friend of the grand old man, Philip Stanhope, presented this proposal to the 1894 interparliamentary conference in Gladstone's name with the result that the plan for such a tribunal was to be forwarded to the member governments. And Alfred Nobel lived to see this happen. But its consequences came after his death : the summoning of the Hague conference and the foundation of the standing court of arbitration there. It is a serious and irreversible loss for the peace movement that men of the calibre of Alfred Nobel, Moritz von Egidy and Johann von Bloch were taken from us so early. It is true that their works and actions live on beyond the grave, but if they were alive among us today their personal influence would give enormous impetus to the movement. How bravely they would have taken up the struggle which is now being initiated by the militarists to maintain the shattered old system.

In vain : the old system must give way when a new one begins to organise itself. The conviction of the possibility, of the necessity and of the rich benefits of a guaranteed peace among the nations on the basis of a system of law has already taken too strong a hold on every section of the national populations, including their leaders, the tasks are laid out too clearly before them, and too many are already working upon them for them not to be achieved sooner or later. Today there are already numerous heads of state who support the ideals of the peace movement. A few years ago not one Minister was among their ranks. The first statesman in power whom I can recall officially declaring his approbation to an interparliamentary conference was the Norwegian Prime Minister Steen. It was John Lund who gave this message—which at the time caused a sensation—to the interparliamentary conference which was meeting in Rome in 1891. The Norwegian government was also the first to approve travel expenses to the members of the Interparliamentary Union and a subsidy to the Bern Peace Bureau. Alfred Nobel did not leave the administration of his peace legacy to the Norwegian Storting without excellent reason.

Let us look about ourselves to ask whether events and situations really justified our talking in terms of the positive achievements of pacifism and of its onward march. A terrible war, such as the world has never seen before, has just been raging in the Far East; it was followed by yet a more terrible revolution which shook the giant Russian empire to its foundations and whose end is not yet in sight. Nothing but fire, sacking, bombs, hangings, overflowing prisons, floggings and massacres—in short, an orgy of satanic power; and in the meantime central and western Europe lives under constant threat of war—with mistrust, threats, the rattling of sabres, persecution campaigns in the press, feverish building of fleets and rearmament everywhere; in England, Germany and France novels are coming out in which attack on a neighbour is seen as a self-evident future occurrence—this is done with the object of inciting an even greater rate of armament; defensive positions are constructed, submarines built, whole stretches mined, airships with military capabilities tested, and all with such zeal as if the next attack were the surest and most important matter for the states, and even the second Hague conference is given an agenda which brands it as a conference of war, and yet people still maintain that the peace movement is making progress?

One should not rest content with looking at the all too evident events on the surface; one should also endeavour to understand what is coming up from beneath; one should understand that two world views and two epochs of civilisation are now in open conflict, and then one will become aware of the fact that in the midst of the crumbling, threatening old order the new order with its promises for the future is struggling into existence, no longer in isolated pockets, no longer weak and disorganised, but already widespread and filled with vigour. Quite independently of the actual peace movement itself, which is more a symptom than a cause of the changes that are taking place, a process of internationalising, of increasing solidarity is taking place in the world. The factors which are contributing to this are the technical inventions, increased communications, the communities of interest branching out and operating on an international level, increased economic interdependence, and—half unaware as instinctive forces are—the drive for self-preservation of human society is present, which is working against the ever-increasing means of destruction which in turn seek to destroy man, and fighting it instinctively.

Alongside these unconscious factors which are preparing the way for an era without war there are those who are fully conscious of the objectives they are pursuing, who already see before them a clear outline of the plan of campaign, who know the techniques and are beginning to apply them, through which the goal that lies before them can be achieved with the greatest despatch. The present English Prime Minister Campbell-Bannerman once more raises the question of disarmament. The French Senator d'Estournelles seeks to pave the way for the Franco-German Entente. Jaurès calls upon the socialists of all countries to come together in united opposition to war. A Russian scholar (Novikow) demands a sevenfold alliance of the confederated great powers of the world; Roosevelt offers arbitration court treaties to all countries and said through his delegation to the congress that it was the duty of every government to employ all possible means to bring nearer the day when the sword will no longer be the arbiter between nations.

I should like to dwell on America for a moment. The land of unlimited opportunities is particularly worthy of note in that it has projected the greatest and newest plans with a bold spirit and knows how to seek out the simplest and most direct means of carrying them out. In other words : idealist in thought, practical in action. The prospect before us is that the modern peace movement will receive a powerful forward impetus from America and a clear formula for the realisation of its aims. In Roosevelt's words referred to above and in the sentences that follow there is a complete grasp of the task which serve for the programme of a current peace campaign being conducted in America, and clearly describes the method :

1. Arbitration court treaties.
2. A peace union between the states.
3. An international institution which can administer justice among the nations, as is done among our states (the USA) and which can eliminate the need for resorting to war.

When Roosevelt received me in the White House on 17 October 1904, he told me that world peace was certainly coming, but it would come little by little.

And it is indeed true. However clearly recognised the goal before us lies, however seemingly close and easily attainable, the path can only be trod one step at a time, and countless obstacles have yet to be overcome.

And above and beyond all other considerations, this is a goal which still lies obscured from many millions, which countless people either know nothing about or which they would regard as a mere Utopia. Powerful interests are at work to seek to prevent its being realised, to keep things as they are. And the proponents of the old, of the status quo, have a powerful ally

indeed in the natural law of inertia which indwells in all things
as a protection against the threat of mortality. So it is no easy
battle which still lies before pacifism. Of all the struggles and
issues which so fill our changing times this question whether
relations between one state and another should be on the basis of
force or justice is the most vital and the most important for the
future. For the happy consequences of a guaranteed world-wide
peace are as inconceivable as would be the consequences of world
war which still threatens, and is still being wished along by
many blinded people. The representatives of pacifism are well
aware of the smallness of their personal influence in real terms,
they know how weak they are in numbers and status, but although they may be modest in their opinion of themselves, they do
not think in modest terms about their cause. They regard it as the
greatest which can ever be served. On its achievement depends
whether Europe is to be the setting of ruin and collapse, or
whether and by what means setting aside this danger will permit
the era of guaranteed peace on the basis of international justice
to be the more readily introduced, in which civilisation will
unfold to unsuspected flowering. That is the question which with
its many aspects was to fill the programme of the second Hague
conference, instead of the proposed discussions on the laws and
customs of war at sea, firing upon harbours, cities and villages,
laying of mines, etc. This programme demonstrates how the
proponents of the present war-based system seek to modify but
still maintain it even on the most private territory of the peace
movement. But the supporters of pacifism, inside and outside the
conference, will be at their posts defending their objectives and
taking yet another step nearer towards them. And that is the
goal which, to repeat Roosevelt's words, represents the obligation
of his, and of all, governments :

"To bring about the day when the judge, not the sword, will
decide among the nations."

SPEECH IN SAN FRANCISCO IN JUNE 1912

Ladies and Gentlemen, Voters of California :

Very often people put the question to me "Do you believe in the possibility of Universal Peace?" It might be taken as a personal slight to be asked if one believes in the thing one lives and works for. But I will not consider the question from the standpoint of faith, because we Pacifists have learned to consider it from the higher standpoint of Science and Law.

Universal Peace is not a question of possibility, but of necessity. It is not only the aim, but the normal condition of civilisation. We must not think we have attained civilisation while we are still loaded with the barbarities of war. The higher organisation of the world must be based on Universal Peace.

All this could be proved by arguments, political, economical and social. These arguments would fill volumes, so I cannot attempt to develop them here. Let me condense my conviction in two sentences.

First. "The development of the doctrine of international arbitration considered from the standpoint of its ultimate benefits to the human race is the most vital movement of modern times."

This sentence is not my own. I quote it from William Howard Taft.

Another sentence from the same source :

"If the United States have a mission, it is to develop the Principle of the Brotherhood of Man into a living palpable force."

The one half of humanity that has never borne arms is today ready to blaze into this living palpable force. Perhaps the Universal Sisterhood is necessary before the Universal Brotherhood is possible.

Everything in America can start right. With us Europeans we are eternally busy shaking off the horrors of the past. You are full of strength and courage, and daring, while we grow old struggling for truth.

The strides you have made for peace and suffrage since I was over here eight years ago, in 1904, are unmeasurable. You are organising the whole country and federating all the branch societies and your executive head is the chief apostle of the movement.

If I tell this to the European audience they not only disbelieve it, but laugh with derision. When people speak to me of the future. I tell them "Go to America and look at the future, for there it has already arrived. They are fifty years in advance of us ethically."

We read in the prophets, "The lion and the lamb shall lie down together and a little child shall lead them." America is the young nation which shall as a regenerated race lead the lion of European militarism and the bleeding lamb of the people to a resting place, a stoppage of these barbarities of armament. The United States must missionise darkest mid-Europe as they have Africa, for in the former the greater dangers are looming. On my way to America through Europe, I was shocked to meet, everywhere, the cry of *war*, and great military manoeuvring going on in every station and capital.

In Paris, the populace was celebrating a religious holiday with shouts of "Vive l'armée," "Down with the Prussian," and the papers were blazing with passionate editorials. English journalism too was recommending conscription and fanning afresh patriotic flames. Alarm is general everywhere and no one can give a rational cause.

In America, the reverse is the truth, you are busy with welfare missions, child-saving, the religious forward movement is re-instilling some of the puritanic ideal; a renaissance of the spirit as it were. Your religious denominations are redoubling their energies to counteract the present-day tendencies toward a lowering of standards. Your reformers and settlement workers are fighting slum evils and labour unrighteousness. In my city they are putting guns into the public schools and making the curriculum less and less liberal, more and more militant.

I am over in America to catch a new breath, to take a hold higher up, to see if I cannot enlist your rank and file to help us.

Hail to the Future! America is the Future embodied so far as my generation shall see it realised! The American people can well afford to glorify their founders and their leaders for what they have wrought for them. Our founders died in the battles for pillage, and our leaders, to our sorrow, are busy planning still other campaigns, while the people hopelessly ask "Who is our enemy; we know no cause for war!"

I have been asked to cross the water by the American women.

They wrote me what can we do to help. I have taken them seriously. I have a definite plan to put before them. I must have their co-operation or yield reluctantly to the up-hill struggle which anti-war ideal is bound to have in a military power. There is but one help and that is an unmuzzled press—a press in the hands of trained independent peace workers who can tell the truth to the enslaved masses, which today are not permitted by the ruling institutions to think but only to shoot, and to shoot each other to uphold their master's prestige.

Our State Church is not the avenue for free discussion. The press is the tool of the War Department. The school gives our boys rifles along with their books.

While the women in California are glorying in their suffrage our men in Hungary are rioting for theirs. We need the enlightment of truth to know our rights before we can attain them, and we can only get that through an honest press. We have already a large body ready to blaze the response to such a voice.

The Peace Movement takes on three distinct aspects.

We consider it as a Religion, as Science, and as a Warfare.

As a Religion it deals with our duties toward God and Man, and appeals through our noblest feelings of Love and Mercy to all that is divine in our souls.

As a Science it bases its arguments on History, on Statistics, on Political Economy, on the natural laws of Harmony and Progress.

As a Warfare it rouses in our hearts the energy for contest, the resolution for victory, the passion of contempt for the lies and the follies and the cruelties of the other side.

As a Religion we preach it; as a Science we teach it; as a Warfare we fight for it.

At the present hour it seems most necessary that we fight for it, for the enemy, I mean the war party, is most vigorously at work just now. Not only rumours of wars, but war itself is upon us, actual strife is being carried on between Italy and Turkey. Alongside the fact of this war which carries so many sparks of danger to bring about a general conflagration, we see the unremitting preparations going on for other wars to come.

We see the spreading of this folly, the epidemic of the age, the contest of armaments on Land, on the Seas and in the Air. So it seems that of the two great unseen powers which are struggling for supremacy the greater chance of this moment is on the side of the evil power.

Those who scoff at the peace movement assume a triumphant attitude, the sceptics lose all courage, and some of the Pacifists themselves prophesy the direst catastrophies for the near future.

The true and convinced peace workers are always optimistic. They are optimistic by nature. They not only wish, they not merely hope, they are certain that the world is progressing, and progressing upwards. They indeed know it. To them the coming peaceful organisation of the world is not merely possible, it is inevitable.

But our optimism does not make us blind to the events of the hour and the dangers of the future. We are not dull to the popular success of our opponents. And because just now, our adversary seems so in the ascendancy, because they have been able to paralyse popular opinion with their threats and their scares, and actually have already loaded their cannons, therefore I believe that it is our task now to fight rather than to teach or to preach.

Certainly their ammunitions seem much stronger than ours. Our public treasuries are their loot; they have the money. They have the men. They have behind them the ambitions of the mighty, the speculations of the greedy, the wild instincts of the ignorant. But never mind. We have behind us the Faith, the Laws of Progress, the Laws of Nature, the Laws of Evolution, the Demands of Humanity; in one word, the Divine Plan has outlined our warfare, and we know the final victory is ours.

I want to draw your attention to one of the enemies' weapons which is most vital now. *I mean the daily press*. It is quite certain that the Italian-Turkish war has been forced upon the government by the public opinion of the country, which in its turn has been swayed by the vigorous campaign of some influential papers. These papers in their turn have been influenced by combined commercial and military powers.

I know in my own country that the War Department has a bureau which furnishes to the daily papers not only information, but leading articles, which perhaps are not intended to push for war, but certainly work to prepare the voters and the parliament to consent to fresh appropriations for the army and the navy and the air fleet.

In passing through Paris I found the strongest war movement on foot. Chauvinism is flooding France. What fans this flame and wakes this voice of war? One need only examine the current press and the answer is clear. In every column there is an essay or an anecdote, or a rumour which either insinuates or openly speaks for war with Germany, and is kindling the military fire-brand.

I noted the contents of one paper out of many. Listen to the headings of the articles and judge for yourself.

The leading editorial was signed by one of the most eloquent members of the French Parliament, of the Clerical Party, Monsieur de Mun. He pleads for a military alliance with England in view of the supremacy of the two countries in the Mediterranean, and speaks as strongly against any conciliation between England and Germany. In the next column is a questionnaire by a French officer. He asks "How will true French women salute their national flag?" The answers of the women are overflowing with patriotic and nationalistic sentiments. The writers seem to think that the only hope of their country is symbolised by the colours, and some express their eagerness to sacrifice their sons.

Next comes the report of a banquet which is given in rejoicing that the downfall of a certain Prefect has been accomplished. The man had been found guilty of protesting against a subscription instigated by military officials for purchasing airships.

Another column has the heading, "Artillery and Aeroplanes".

Now if war should come about between France and Germany the largest credit of it would certainly be due to the efforts of the daily press. This instrument is evidently the most efficient to mould the public spirit. After the long experience I have had as to the results of propaganda work I have come to the conclusion that the one thing needful to make a sentiment prevail is the daily paper.

Yet, let me emphasise that on our continent too, in spite of the reactionary forces which work to uphold the old barbaric order, other forces are mightily pushing forward to bring in the new order of Peace and Justice.

So the labour parties and all the Socialists firmly oppose every war and every increase of armaments (but alas, in official circles they are not listened to).

Among the teachers and students the ideals of the Peace movement are fast gaining ground (but alas, the Department of Public Instruction only pursue the cultivation of local patriotism).

And in wide circles of the intelligent classes, among the learned, the poets, the artists, the peace movement possesses its daily increasing number of adherents and zealous defenders.

Europe is the cradle of the Interparliamentary Union, and the nucleus of the future peace order as a legal institution is to be found on the old continent. I mean the Tribunal of the Hague.

You are fully aware what this Tribunal signifies. You have also heard here, in Los Angeles, one of its great workers, Baron d'Estournelles, report about the history and the results of those remarkable Conferences.

But what Baron d'Estournelles could not tell you—because he would not speak in his own praise—let me add.

I was present at The Hague and saw him at work. He was one of the pillars of the Conference.

He was among the great spirits who saved its work from the hands of the opposition within the camp, which had been sent as representatives by several of the Powers, who had no concept of Peace. He was the author of Article 27, declaring that recourse to Arbitration in cases of quarrel should be considered as a duty on the part of all Governments.

His biggest backing came from the American delegation, which in its turn was encouraged by the demonstrations of the American people. Letters and petitions poured in from the States and were communicated to the entire assembly. Yours was the only Nation that sent in its public opinion to sway the Conferences.

After the establishment of the Hague Tribunal, Baron d' Estournelles achieved another great step. This Tribunal and its laws had been instituted somewhat against the good-will of certain signing Powers, and their desire was, perhaps, to let the infant die which they had helped so weakly to animate. By them the organism was not expected to function. Baron d' Estournelles, however, grasped this crisis and he proceeded to the United States. He best knew where help was to be had. He appealed to your President and asked him to put the first case before this Tribunal, that its wheels might be set in motion. Theodore Roosevelt did not hesitate. An old question lying in the State Department with regard to Mexican church funds was taken out of the dusty portfolios and was officially laid before the Hague Tribunal as the first International question to be solved by it. So my friend, Baron d'Estournelles, with the aid of the Americans kept the infant breathing, and you certainly know how many wars have since been averted through this Heaven-sent institution. I need only to allude to the Morocco question which can never threaten us again, for all its future details and differences must come before The Hague.

You will be interested in a little personal reminiscence which shows another side of the American keenness to help internationally.

In 1904 I was received at the White House. Your energetic National business manager, the President, Theodore Roosevelt, received me, and knowing what my interests were naturally discussed with me the Peace question. He promised to try to do his best for the cause. We simple mortals are accustomed to such promises from official places, and know how they generally end. Men in power usually say, "We shall see what can be done", but they are quite as usually too busy to see, and most of the time nothing is done. But this case was different.

Mr. Roosevelt is not given to making vague statements. He promised me three definite things. He said "I will propose arbitration treaties to every European Power, also to your Austria".

"I will take the initiative and call a second Hague Conference."

"I will try to put a stop to the hateful war between Japan and Russia."

History records that he kept these three promises.

Shaking hands with me at parting, he said these ever remembered words. "Be sure Universal Peace is coming, because it is bound to come, but only step by step."

THE STRUGGLE TO PREVENT WAR

August 1893: On this occasion again the newspapers have been grievously in error. When such a conflict situation emerges, thousands upon thousands of petty journalists believe themselves called upon to speak out in the name of their country. "We shall truly show who we are—we shall not yield—we shall not lose one foot of our native soil—" and much more of the like. The left bank of the Mekon suddenly became the dearest personal prize of every manjack of these journalists. And all the arrogance, aggression, lust for conquest which has manifest itself on this occasion has not unnaturally aroused wrath and indignation among many people abroad. . . . It is all too easily forgotten that it is not a nation that conducts foreign policy, but a few individuals in the ministerial and press offices. Wherever the idea of a nation appears in abstract terms it is always in a most repugnant aspect : self-congratulation, lust for power, injustice, greed—these are just a few characteristics of these phantoms floating in the air saluting one another with wild grimaces.

August 1894: And on the subject of China, which has now become the focal point of attention : China regards itself as the sole legitimate sovereign state to which all other states owe tribute. If it were to acquire a taste for warmongering it might perhaps consider attacking Europe and making the theoretically tributary states into real subject states. And if the people of the west were not united, how would they be able to ward off such an invasion? It is no answer to say "This is why we must arm." There is a world of difference between civilised states coming together in an armed federation against predatory attack and individual states having their whole populations armed against one another and on a war footing.

July 1898: As these lines were going to press the news came of Bismarck's death. I wonder if the statesman has yet been born who will achieve for the idea of humanity what Bismarck achieved for the idea of the German nation?

June 1907 : In Austria universal suffrage has been introduced and by excluding the extreme nationalist parties only the red and the black will be represented in the new parliament. In these notes I usually refrain from comment on internal Austrian political affairs. This democratisation—more than that, this social democratisation of our feudal military state—is a real step forward in the context of the general social changes in our time and should therefore be noted here.

April 1911 : In Vienna the women workers organised a mass demonstration in favour of votes for women. They marched through the streets in their thousands, but in an orderly and peaceful fashion. Adelheid Popp said, "But we also want to fight against the fact that millions are squandered on murderous ends and in setting brother against brother. We want an end to armament, to the means of murder and we want these millions to be applied to meet the needs of the people!" Feminine politics? No : humane politics. And the time is fast approaching in which the well-being and the rights of mankind will be regarded as the highest political yardstick; this early initiative by the one half of humanity which up to now has been deprived of all rights is just one of the symptoms.

February 1912 : Between which two European powers would war not be a crime today? Or an unspeakable catastrophe? From all the dangerous groupings and shifts of alliances of the various states there emerges ever more clearly one fundamental necessity, which must be proclaimed to all and striven towards as a concrete political objective of pacifism : namely, bringing all the separate alliances together into a European customs and defence union. Pan-European union. Not on the model of the United States, where there is a single central government, but on the pattern of the Union of American republics in which each state preserves its independence and equality with others.

April 1914: It is said—but it is not yet official—that the next Hague conference is to be postponed until 1917. If the unavoidable great European war, so confidently predicted by the lovers of war for every "thaw", is avoided for that length of time and the idea of peace is strengthened in the interim period, with the result that an overwhelming number of the people desirous of peace were sent to the conference, the conference itself would be able to bring about the creation of a permanent court of arbitration and not just a standstill, but automatic reduction in armaments.

May 1914: A German aeroplane crossed the Russian frontier and landed in the province of Perm. The airmen were arrested and sentenced to prison. For flying over frontiers is against the law in Russia, and therefore it is a crime. We live in the "age of transport". Why isn't crossing the frontier by foot or by road or by rail forbidden? Answer: because the customs posts offer guarantees—and anyway aircraft are particularly dangerous on account of spying; it seems that customs barriers and the secrets of the military are at odds with the newest achievement of the genius of man. But the question now is: Which is now to give way under these new conditions, the exploitation of human achievement or the customs and military defensive system?

SOURCES TO THE TRANSLATIONS

How I came to write "Lay down your Arms".—Stimmen und Gestalten, Leipzig, 1907, p. 105ff.

Lay down your Arms.—T. Holmes (trans.), *Lay down your Arms*, 2nd. ed., London, 1894. This edition is described as the "authorised translation . . . revised by the authoress".

Memories of Alfred Nobel.—Stimmen und Gestalten, Leipzig, 1907, p. 135ff.

The next Peace Congress in Rome.—Neue Freie Presse, 3 September 1891. A prefatory editorial note in the original expresses pleasure in putting space at the disposal of this famous authoress for the purpose of this appeal on behalf of the peace movement.

The Development of the Peace Movement.—Speech to the Nobel Committee of Storting, 18 April 1906. Quoted from *Les Prix Nobel en 1905*, Stockholm, 1907, p. 1ff.

Speech in San Francisco in June 1912. Original typescript in English from the Collection Suttner-Fried (XYc II) in the Library of the United Nations, Geneva. The text is presented as it stands, apart from a few minor spelling and punctuation changes.

The Struggle to prevent World War.—Der Kampf um die Vermeidung des Weltkrieges, Zurich, 1917.

BIBLIOGRAPHY OF BERTHA SUTTNER'S WRITINGS

Inventarium einer Seele, W. Friedrich, Leipzig, 1883.

Ein Manuskript!, W. Friedrich, Leipzig, 1884.

Ein schlechter Mensch, O. Heinrichs, Munich, 1885.

Daniela Dormes, O. Heinrichs, Munich, 1886.

High Life, O. Heinrichs, Munich, 1886.

Verkettungen, W. Friedrich, Leipzig, 1887.

Inventarium einer Seele, 2nd ed. W. Friedrich, Leipzig, 1888.

Schriftstellerroman, E. Pierson, Dresden, 1888.

Erzählte Lustspiele. Neues aus dem High Life, E. Pierson, Dresden, 1889.

Die Waffen nieder! Eine Lebensgeschichte, E. Pierson, Dresden, 1889.

Erzählungen und Betrachtungen, Österr-ung. Volksbücher, Vienna, 1890.

Das Maschinenzeitalter, Zukunftsvorlesungen über unsere Zeit von "Jemand" 2nd ed. Verlags-Magazin, Zurich, 1891.

Ein Manuskript!, 2nd ed. E. Pierson, Dresden, 1892.

Doctor Hellmuts Donnerstage, E. Pierson, Dresden, 1892.

An der Riviera, J. Bensheimer's V., Mannheim, 1892.

Eva Siebeck, E. Pierson, Dresden, 1892.

Inventarium einer Seele, 3rd ed. E. Pierson, Dresden, 1892.

Verkettungen, E. Pierson, Dresden, 1892.

Im Berghause, A. Goldschmidt, Berlin, 1893.

Phantasien über den "Gotha", E. Pierson, Dresden, 1893.

Die Tiefinnersten, E. Pierson, Dresden, 1893.

Trente et quarante!, E. Pierson, Dresden, 1893.

Es Löwos, eine Monographie, E. Pierson, Dresden, 1894 (first appeared in the periodical "Die Gesellschaft", Munich, 1885).

Vor dem Gewitter, Raimund und Chodina, Vienna, 1894.

Hanna, E. Pierson, Dresden, 1894.

Erzählte Lustspiele, 3rd ed., E. Pierson, Dresden, 1895.

Ein Manuskript, 3rd ed., E. Pierson, Dresden, 1895.

Eva Siebeck, 3rd ed., E. Pierson, Dresden, 1895.

Die Waffen nieder!, Eine Lebensgeschichte, 12th thousand, E. Pierson, Dresden, 1895.

Krieg und Frieden, Erzählungen, Aphorismen, Betrachtungen, collected and edited by L. Katscher, Rosenbaum and H., Berlin, 1896.

Nabucco, dram. Gedicht in 4 Aufzügen von Ferdinand Fontana, translated by B. v. S., E. Pierson, Dresden, 1896.

Einsam und arm, E. Pierson, Dresden, 1896.

Frühlingszeit, Lenzes- und Lebensgabe unseren erwachsenen Töchtern zur Unterhaltung und Belehrung gewidmet von den deutschen Dichterinnen der Gegenwart, J. Gnadenfeld & Co., Stuttgart, 1896.

High Life, 2nd ed., E. Pierson, Dresden, 1896.

Die Waffen nieder! Eine Lebensgeschichte, 14th ed., E. Pierson, Dresden, 1896.

Die Waffen nieder! Eine Lebensgeschichte, Popular ed., 1896.

Die Waffen nieder! Eine Lebensgeschichte, edited for young people by H. Gräfin Pötting, 1896.

Der Kaiser von Europa, based on the English of F. A. Fawkes, Vita, Berlin, 1897.

Schmetterlinge, Novellen und Skizzen, E. Pierson, Dresden, 1897.

La Traviata (new edition of "An der Riviera"), E. Pierson, Dresden, 1898.

Schriftstellerroman, 2nd ed., E. Pierson, Dresden, 1898.

Ku-i-kuk, Niemals eine Zweite, Kürschners Bücherschatz, 1899.

Schach der Qual, ein Phantasiestück, 5th ed., E. Pierson, Dresden, 1899.

Herrn Dr. Carl Freiherr v. Stengals u. andere Argumente für und wider den Krieg von Dr. N. N. Privat Docent an der Universität..., edited by Bertha von Suttner, Vienna, 1899.

Die Waffen nieder! Eine Lebensgeschichte, 29th ed., E. Pierson, Dresden, 1899.

Daniela Dormes, 2nd ed., E. Pierson, Dresden, 1900.

Die Haager Friedenskonferenz, Tagebuchblätter, E. Pierson, Dresden, 1900.

Krieg und Frieden, Vortrag, A. Schupp, Munich, 1900.

Das Maschinenzeitalter, Zukunftsvorlesungen über unsere Zeit, 3rd ed., E. Pierson, Dresden, 1899.

Ein schlechter Mensch, 2nd ed., E. Pierson, Dresden, 1900.

Die Haager Friedenskonferenz, Tagebuchblätter, 2nd ed., E. Pierson, Dresden, 1901.

High Life, 3rd ed., E. Pierson, Dresden, 1902.

Marthas Kinder, Fortsetzung zu "Die Waffen nieder", E. Pierson, Dresden, 1902.

Vor dem Gewitter, 2nd ed., E. Pierson, Dresden, 1903.

Marthas Kinder, 5th–10th ed., E. Pierson, Dresden, 1904, 1905.

Briefe an einen Toten, 4th–6th ed., E. Pierson, Dresden, 1904, 1905.

Inventarium einer Seele, 4th ed., E. Pierson, Dresden, 1904.

Ketten und Verkettungen, Donna Sol, M. Hesses Volksbücherei, Leipzig, 1904.

Erzählte Lustspiele, M. Hesses Volksbücherei Nr. 250–251, Leipzig, 1905.

Babies 7. Liebe u. Anderes, Neue Folge der "Erzählten Lustspiele" 1st–3rd ed., E. Pierson, Dresden, 1905.

Die Waffen nieder! Eine Lebensgeschichte, 37th ed., E. Pierson, Dresden, 1905.

Die Waffen nieder! Eine Lebensgeschichte, Popular ed., 1st–40th thousand, E. Pierson, 1905.

Bertha von Suttners gesammelte Schriften in 12 Bdn., E. Pierson, Dresden, 1906.

Frühlingszeit (new edition), Globus Verlag, Berlin, 1906.

Randglossen zur Zeitgeschichte, Das Jahr 1905, C. Siwinna, Kattowitz, 1906.

Die Waffen nieder! Eine Lebensgeschichte, Popular ed., 51st–60th thousand, E. Pierson, 1906.

Marthas Kinder, Popular ed., 1st–20th Tausend, E. Pierson, 1906.

Stimmen und Gestalten, B. Elischer Nachfolger, Leipzig, 1907.

Zur nächsten intergouvernementalen Konferenz im Haag, W. Süsserott, Berlin, 1907.

Randglossen zur Zeitgeschichte, Das Jahr 1906, C. Siwinna, Kattowitz, 1907.

Inventarium einer Seele (Popular ed.), E. Pierson, Dresden, 1908.

Schriftstellerroman (Popular ed.), E. Pierson, Dresden, 1908.

Eva Siebeck (Popular ed.), E. Pierson, Dresden, 1908.

La Traviata (Popular ed.), E. Pierson, Dresden, 1908.

Memoiren, Deutsche Verlags-Anstalt, Stuttgart, 1909.

Einsam und arm (Popular ed.), Berlin-Wien Verlag, Berlin, 1909.

Schach der Qual, ein Phantasiestück (Popular ed.), Berlin-Wien Verlag, Berlin, 1909.

Phantasien über den Gotha (Popular ed.), Berlin-Wien Verlag, Berlin, 1909.

Rüstung und Überrüstung, Hesperus Verlag, Berlin, 1909.

Der Menschheit Hochgedanken, Roman aus der nächsten Zukunft, Verlag der "Friedens-Warte", Berlin, 1911.

Die Barbarisierung der Luft, Internationale Verständigung, Heft 6, Verlag der "Friedens-Warte", Berlin, 1912.

Aus der Werkstatt des Pazifismus (Aus der eigenen Werkstatt Bd. 2, Vortragszyklus) H. Heller u. Co., Vienna, 1912.

Ku-i-kuk, Universal Bibliothek 5568, Leipzig, 1913.

Die Waffen nieder! Eine Lebensgeschichte, Popular ed., 191st–210th thousand, Verlag Berlin-Wien, Berlin, 1914.

Der Kampf um die Vermeidung des Weltkrieges, Randglossen aus zwei Jahrzehnten zu den Ereignissen vor der Katastrophe (1892–1900, 1907–1914), edited by Dr. Alfred H. Fried, Orell Füssli, Zurich, 1917.

INDEX OF NAMES